Contents

I0160546

Chapter One ~ Conflict in the Cosmos

There Was War In The Heavens

"*And there was war in heaven. Michael and his angels fought against the dragon, and the dragon and his angels fought back, but he was not strong enough, and they lost their place in heaven. The great dragon was hurled down — that ancient serpent called the devil, or Satan, who leads the whole world astray. He was hurled to the earth, and his angels with him*" (Rev 12:7-9).

1

Lucifer's Heavenly Role:

Prior to the outbreak of this conflict in the heavens, Satan -- referred to here as the devil, the serpent and the dragon -- was one of the covering cherubs, guarding the throne of God Almighty. Satan's name, prior to his rebellion, was Lucifer, which translated literally, means the light-bearer, or standard-bearer of the colors. The prophet, Ezekiel, describes Lucifer's original angelic status as follows: *"Thus saith the Lord Jehovah: Thou sealest up the sum, full of wisdom, and perfect in beauty.* **Thou wast in Eden, the garden of God; every precious stone was thy covering, the sardius, the topaz, and the diamond, the beryl, the onyx, and the jasper, the sapphire, the emerald, and the carbuncle, and gold: the workmanship of thy tabrets and of thy pipes was in thee***; in the day that thou wast created they were prepared. Thou wast the anointed cherub that covereth: and I set thee, (so that) thou wast upon the holy mountain of God;* **thou hast walked up and down in the midst of the stones of fire***. Thou wast perfect in thy ways from the day that thou wast created, till unrighteousness was found in thee"* (Ezek 28:12-15).

Lucifer was the model of perfection, dwelling in Eden, the Garden of God. He was adorned with precious stones mounted in gold -- stones that represented authority, under God, over all His created works. He was also 'fitted with tabrets and pipes'. The precious stones, are mentioned here are also identified by Moses, who on Mount Sinai, was told that he was to create a model after the pattern of the things in heaven (Ex 25).

Precious Stones:

*"The LORD said to Moses, "Tell the Israelites to bring me an offering. You are to receive the offering for me from each man whose heart prompts him to give. These are the offerings you are to receive from them: gold, silver and bronze; blue, purple and scarlet yarn and fine linen; goat hair; ram skins dyed red and hides of sea cows; acacia wood; olive oil for the light; spices for the anointing oil and for the fragrant incense; and **onyx stones and other gems to be mounted on the ephod and breastpiece**"* (Ex 25:1-7).

*"And thou shalt make the rational of judgment with embroidered work of diverse colors, according to the workmanship of the ephod, of gold, violet, and purple, and scarlet twice dyed, and fine twisted linen. It shall be four square and doubled: it shall be the measure of a span both in length and in breadth. **And thou shalt set in it four rows of stones. In the first row shall be a sardius stone, and a topaz, and an emerald: In the second a carbuncle, a sapphire, and a jasper: In the third a ligurius, an agate, and an amethyst: In the fourth a chrysolite, an onyx, and a beryl. They shall be set in gold by their rows. And they shall have the names of the children of Israel: with twelve names shall they be engraved, each stone with the name of one according to the twelve tribes**"* (Ex 28:15-21).

According to the Jewish Encyclopedia: The vestments of the high priest were interpreted in three ways. The explanation of historian Philo is as follows:

"His upper garment was the symbol of the ether, while the blossoms represented the earth, the pomegranates typified running water, and the bells denoted the music of the water.

The ephod corresponded to heaven, and the stones on both shoulders to the two hemispheres,one above and the other below the earth. The six names on each of the stones were the six signs of the zodiac, which were denoted also by the twelve names on the breastplate. *The miter was the sign of the crown which exalted the high priest above all earthly kings.*

Josephus' explanation is this: *The ephod typified the four elements, and the interwoven gold denoted the glory of God. The breastplate was in the center of the ephod, as the earth formed the center of the universe; the girdle symbolized the ocean, the stones on the shoulders the sun and moon, and the jewels in the breastplate the twelve signs of the zodiac, while the miter was a token of heaven.*

St. Thomas Aquinas, in his "Summa Theologica" wrote: *According to some, the literal reason for these vestments was that they denoted the disposition of the terrestrial globe; as though the high-priest confessed himself to be the minister of the Creator of the world, wherefore it is written* (Wis. 18:24): ***"In the robe" of Aaron "was the whole world" described.*** *For the linen breeches signified the earth out of which the flax grows. The surrounding belt signified the ocean which surrounds the earth. The violet tunic denoted the air by its color: its little bells betoken the thunder; the pomegranates, the lightning.*

The ephod, by its many colors, signified the starry heaven; the two onyx stones denoted the two hemispheres, or the sun and moon. The twelve precious stones on the breast are the twelve signs of the zodiac: and they are said to have been placed on the rational because in heaven, are the types [rationes] of earthly things, *according to Job 38:33: "Dost thou know the order of heaven, and canst thou set down the reason [rationale] thereof on the earth?" The turban or tiara signified the empyrean: the golden plate was a token of God, the governor of the universe.*

In John the Revelator's vision of the Heavenly Jerusalem, the City stands on a foundation of twelve stones, each correlating with one of the stones of the breast plate, or ephod. However, the foundation stones of the New Jerusalem are in a different order than in the ephod -- with the last stone of the breastplate (the stone associated with the tribe of Benjamin) listed first.

"And the foundations of the wall of the city were adorned with all manner of precious stones. The first foundation was jasper: the second, sapphire: the third; a chalcedony: the fourth, an emerald: The fifth, sardonyx: the sixth, sardius: the seventh, chrysolite: the eighth, beryl: the ninth, a topaz: the tenth, a chrysoprasus: the eleventh, a jacinth: the twelfth, an amethyst. And the twelve gates are twelve pearls, one to each: and every several gate was of one several pearl. And the street of the city was pure gold, as it were, transparent glass" (Rev 21:19-21).

The Golden Garments (8th) of the Kohen Gadol Shemot 28:4:42

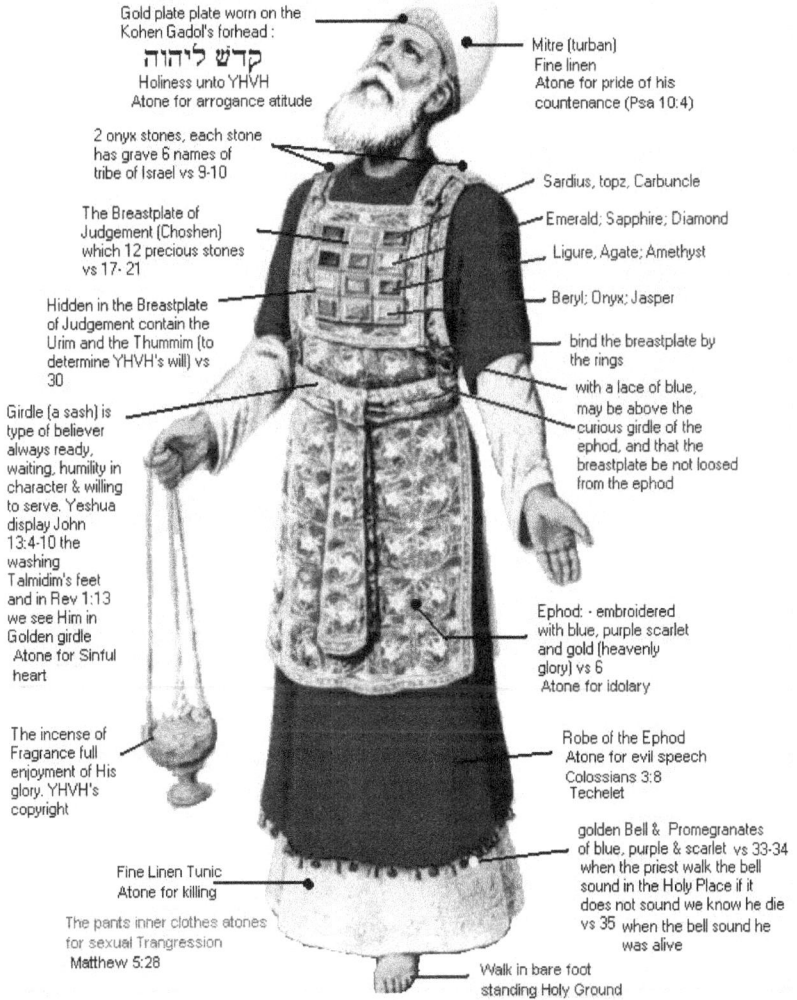

Gold plate plate worn on the Kohen Gadol's forhead :

קדש ליהוה

Holiness unto YHVH
Atone for arrogance atitude

Mitre (turban)
Fine linen
Atone for pride of his countenance (Psa 10:4)

2 onyx stones, each stone has grave 6 names of tribe of Israel vs 9-10

Sardius, topz, Carbuncle

The Breastplate of Judgement (Choshen) which 12 precious stones vs 17- 21

Emerald; Sapphire; Diamond

Ligure, Agate; Amethyst

Hidden in the Breastplate of Judgement contain the Urim and the Thummim (to determine YHVH's will) vs 30

Beryl; Onyx; Jasper

bind the breastplate by the rings

with a lace of blue, may be above the curious girdle of the ephod, and that the breastplate be not loosed from the ephod

Girdle (a sash) is type of believer always ready, waiting, humility in character & willing to serve. Yeshua display John 13:4-10 the washing Talmidim's feet and in Rev 1:13 we see Him in Golden girdle
Atone for Sinful heart

The incense of Fragrance full enjoyment of His glory. YHVH's copyright

Ephod: - embroidered with blue, purple scarlet and gold (heavenly glory) vs 6
Atone for idolary

Robe of the Ephod
Atone for evil speech
Colossians 3:8
Techelet

golden Bell & Promegranates of blue, purple & scarlet vs 33-34 when the priest walk the bell sound in the Holy Place if it does not sound we know he die vs 35 when the bell sound he was alive

Fine Linen Tunic
Atone for killing

The pants inner clothes atones for sexual Trangression
Matthew 5:28

Walk in bare foot standing Holy Ground

The significance of the breastplate, is that of Divine truth shining forth from Divine good, expressed in ultimates progressively from the inmost things in the heavens. The ephod represents the ultimates within the spiritual kingdom, and therefore the ultimates of heaven.

The breast plate had this signification because it was fastened upon the breast where the heart is, and was filled with precious stones. The heart corresponds to celestial good, which represents the love of the Lord for His creation. The twelve precious stones correspond to Divine truths thence derived. Hence the breastplate, in a supreme sense signifies Divine truth shining forth from the Divine good of the Lord.

The twelve stones were inlaid in the Ephod of the Hakohen Hagadol -- these twelve stones representing the twelve Tribes -- one stone for each Tribe. Each of the stones had a name of one of the twelve Tribes of Israel engraved on it, and each, as the writings of St. Thomas Aquinas indicate, was associated with one of the Mazzaroth symbols (Signs of the Zodiac). While there are endless variations as to which Zodiac sign goes with what Tribe, the most reliable seems to be those mentioned in Bullinger's "The Witness of the Stars" (1893). The stones were inlaid in gold representing purity, and the ephod was mounted on royal blue cloth, representing Divine Wisdom.

In the early Church era, Andreas of Cappadocia Caesarea (AD 431-506), relying on (Rev 21:14) associated each of the foundation stones of the New Jerusalem with one of the Apostles. He included Paul among them, but omitted James the Greater, and, naturally, replaced Judas with Matthias. The Tribe of Joseph is sometimes not counted, and the Tribe of Levi is often not counted as a separate Tribe. In their places, the Tribes headed by Joseph's sons, Mannaseh and Ephraim, are counted).

According to Ezekiel's vision, Lucifer, in addition to being adorned with precious stones, had other attributes. The King James Version says, "**the workmanship of thy tabrets and of thy pipes was in thee.**" This obscure passage, while difficult to understand from the King James' version, has been completely removed from many modern translations, including the NIV. Regrettably, this has resulted in the church missing Lucifer's nature, his attributes and inherent abilities to deceive the children of God.

To better understand this, we refer back to the original Hebrew text. Commencing in verse 12, we read: "The Lord said thus unto him: ['Ataah chowteem taakniyt maalee' chaak'maah uwkliyl yopiy], meaning (*You sum up, or consummate, the fullness of skill, wisdom and beauty, perfectly*). [B-Eeden gan Elohiym haayiytaa], meaning (*In Eden -- Adam's home -- the garden of the Divine Magistrates -- you existed*). [Kaal- 'eben y qaaraah m cukaatekaa], meaning (*every, or all, precious stones, your garniture, ornament, or covering*).

After this, are listed the precious stones followed by that part omitted from many versions.

[m le'ket tupeykaa uwnqaabeykaa baak B yowm hibaara'kaa kownaanuw], meaning (*your deputyship, or ministry of tabret, timbrel and tamborine and pipes, the instruments within you, were formed in the day you were created perfect*). ['At-kruwb mimshach hacowkeek uwntatiykaa Bhar qodesh Elohiym], meaning (*You are a cherub, anointed, and I have given you charge over, to protect, the hallowed mountain of The Supreme Ones*). [haayiytaa Btowk 'abneey-'eesh hithalaaktaa], meaning (*It came to pass -- or it was so that -- among the fiery stones you have walked*). [Taamiym 'ataah bidraakeykaa miyowm hibaar'aak 'ad-mimtssa 'aw;aataah baak], meaning (*Morally perfect -- sound and without blemish -- you were, in your course, or mode, of life; from the time you were created, until there appeared perverseness within you*).

Putting this all together, we read: "*You sum up, or consummate, the fullness of skill, wisdom and beauty, perfectly. In Eden -- Adam's home -- the garden of the Divine Magistrates -- you existed. Every, or all, precious stones, (were) your garniture, vestiture, ornamentation, or covering. ... [the stones are listed here] ... your deputyship, or ministry of tabret, timbrel and tamborine and pipes, the instruments within you, were formed in the day you were created perfect. You are a cherub, anointed, and I have given you charge over, to protect, the hallowed mountain of The Supreme Ones. It came to pass -- or it was so that -- among the fiery stones you have walked. Morally perfect -- sound and without blemish -- you were, in your course, or mode, of life; from the time you were created, until there appeared perverseness within you.*"

Based on this translation, the attributes of Lucifer included these:
- He was created perfect, [1]
- He was the sum, the consummate fullness, of skill, wisdom and knowledge,
- He dwelt in Eden, the Garden of God,
- He was arrayed in priestly vestiture, including the breastplate, or ephod, that had mounted upon it, precious stones -- the colors of which form a perfect rainbow, [2]
- He was the deputy, or director, over the heavenly praise and worship -- having created within him, the music of tabret, timbrel, tamborine, and pipes (wind instruments), [3]
- He was a cherub, anointed and given charge over -- commissioned to protect -- the hallowed mountain of the Supreme Ones, [4]

7

- He walked among the fiery stones, [5]
- He was morally perfect -- sound and without blemish in his lifestyle, from the moment he was created, until perverseness, or iniquity, appeared in him. [6]

[1] Lucifer was created perfect. Some have suggested that he was intentionally created as the accuser and destroyer, citing (Is 54:16), which being poorly translated in the KJV, reads: *"It is I who have created the destroyer to work havoc."* This translation is inconsistent with the next verse which says, *"No weapon forged against you will prevail, and you will refute every tongue that accuses you."* Referring to the Hebrew once more, this apparent contradiction is easily resolved.

The Hebrew reads [baaraa'tiy mashchiyt lchabeel kliy], which more properly is translated (*I have cut down, or dispatched, the destroyer, who is an instrument of destruction*). Only this translation is consistent with the remainder of verse 17, that reads: *"This is the heritage of the servants of the Lord, and this is their vindication from me, declares the Lord."*

[2] Lucifer's Failure -- When the description of Lucifer provided by Ezekiel is compared with the pattern of heavenly things revealed to Moses on Mount Sinai, it is clear that Lucifer was arrayed in the vestiture of the high priest. The colors of the stones in his breastplate, or ephod, like those in the ephod worn by the high priests of Israel, form a perfect rainbow, the symbol of the promises of God. Lucifer's apparel, combined with his commission discussed under [4], make it clear that prior to his fall, Lucifer stood before The Omnipotent Ones, as high priest whose functions were to guard the throne of God, serve as the standard bearer of the sacred colors, lead the heavenly choir, and protect and care for The Divine Family.

One of Lucifer's notable characteristics involved his musical talents, which are covered in greater detail under item [3] below. However, it is important to note here that the musicians in Israel were all Levites -- part of the priesthood. *"Those who were musicians (were) heads of Levite families ... and were exempt from other duties because they were responsible for this work day and night"* (1 Ch 9:33). *"All the Levites who were musicians ... stood on the east side of the altar, dressed in fine linen and playing cymbals, harps and lyres. They were accompanied by 120 priests sounding trumpets; and the trumpeters and singers joined in unison, as with one voice, to give praise and thanks to the Lord. ... They raised their voices in praise to the Lord and sang: "He is good; His love endures forever."*

"Then the temple of the Lord was filled with a cloud, and the priests could not perform their service because of the cloud, for the glory of the Lord filled the temple of God" (2 Ch 5:12).

Heavenly Harmony:
Lucifer and the other angels were created before man. He was one of the 'sons of the morning' (Is 14:12; Job 1:6; 2:1). He was, as noted from Ezekiel 28:12-15, the director of ministry. The fact that Lucifer existed prior to man, is attested by the conversation between Job and God, when God inquired of Job: *"Where were you when I laid the earth's foundation? Tell me, if you understand. Who marked off its dimensions? Surely you know! Who stretched a measuring line across it? On what were its footings set, or who laid its cornerstone — while the morning stars sang together and all the angels shouted for joy?"* (Job 38:4-7).

From this Scripture, it would appear that when the foundations of the earth were laid, there was still perfect harmony in heaven since the morning stars -- presumably including Lucifer -- sang together, and *all* the angels shouted for joy. Perverseness apparently, had not yet entered into Lucifer's heart. What caused this dramatic change in Lucifer, transforming him from the covering cherub anointed and appointed as the director of the heavenly music ministry, into Satan, the destroyer? What destroyed the heavenly harmony, resulting in division among the angels, culminating in battles between Michael and his angels, and Lucifer and his? In time, we will reveal the answer.

The Levitical Priesthood -- A Shadow of Things to Come:
After Lucifer's fall, and the subsequent fall of man, there was a time when each man did what seemed right in his own eyes (Dt 12:8). Then, some time later, during Abram's lifetime, there was a high priest who ruled over the Canaanites, called Melchizedek, identified as the priest of God Most High (Gen 14:18). After God delivered Israel out of Egypt, He restored the priesthood, but this priesthood -- the Levitical Priesthood -- was inferior to the Melchizedek priesthood, being a shadow of things to come, the reality of which was to be found in the person of Yeshua Messiah, Christ Jesus (Col 2:17).

During this era, the role of high priest, was temporarily carried out by Israel's high priest. These shadows of things to come, were fulfilled, or brought into reality, in Christ -- a member of the Godhead -- when Christ became incarnate in human flesh. *"Christ Jesus: Who, being in the form of God, thought it not robbery to be equal with God: But made himself of no reputation, and took upon him the form of a servant, and was made in the likeness of*

"Men. And being found in fashion as a man, he humbled himself, and became obedient unto death, even the death of the cross. Wherefore God also hath highly exalted him, and given him a name which is above every name: That at the name of Jesus every knee should bow, of things in heaven, and things in earth, and things under the earth; And that every tongue should confess that Jesus Christ is Lord, to the glory of God the Father"* (Phil 2:5-11).

Christ not only set aside his divinity to become a man. He not only took upon himself the very nature of a servant -- to serve others. He not only died for them in their stead (Phil 2:5-8); Christ ultimately fulfilled the priestly role originally assigned to Lucifer -- now Satan -- whose very purpose and intent had now become to destroy Christ, his Creator, and elevate himself above God! Concerning this, the prophet, Isaiah, wrote:

"How you have fallen from heaven, O morning star, son of the dawn! You have been cast down to the earth, you who once laid low the nations! You said in your heart, "I will ascend to heaven; I will raise my throne above the stars of God; I will sit enthroned on the mount of assembly, on the utmost heights of the sacred mountain. I will ascend above the tops of the clouds; I will make myself like the Most High." But you are brought down to the grave, to the depths of the pit" (Is 14:12-15).

Christ (The Anointed One) Our High Priest:

Christ became our High Priest. The author of the Book of Hebrews says: *"Therefore, since we have a great high priest who has gone through the heavens, Jesus the Son of God, let us hold firmly to the faith we profess"* (Heb 4:14-15). ... *"Christ also did not take upon himself the glory of becoming a high priest. "But God said to him, "You are my Son; today I have become your Father." And he says in another place, "You are a priest forever, in the order of Melchizedek"* (Heb 5:5-6). ... *"Although he was a son, he learned obedience from what he suffered and, once made perfect, he became the source of eternal salvation for all who obey him and was designated by God to be high priest in the order of Melchizedek"* (Heb 5:8-10).

"Jesus, who went before us, has entered on our behalf. He has become a high priest forever, in the order of Melchizedek" (Heb 6:20). ... *"We do have such a high priest, who sat down at the right hand of the throne of the Majesty in heaven, and who serves in the sanctuary, the true tabernacle set up by the Lord, not by man"* (Heb 8:1-2).

"When Christ came as high priest of the good things that are already here, he went through the greater and more perfect tabernacle that is not man-made, that is to say, not a part of this creation. He did not enter by means of the blood of goats and calves; but he entered the Most Holy Place once for all by his own blood, having obtained eternal redemption" (Heb 9:11-12). ... *"Through Jesus, therefore, let us continually offer to God a sacrifice of praise — the fruit of lips that confess his name. And do not forget to do good and to share with others, for with such sacrifices God is pleased"* (Heb 13:15-16).

A Continuing Priesthood:

"And Jesus holds his priesthood permanently, because he continues forever. Consequently, he is able to save to the uttermost those who draw near to God through him, since he always lives to make intercession for them. For it is indeed fitting that we should have such a high priest, holy, innocent, unstained, separated from sinners, and exalted above the heavens" (Heb 7:24-26).

11

Lucifer's Final Punishment:
When Christ has completed his role as advocate and high priest of the people before the throne of God, then will be carried out that drama symbolized by the destiny of the scapegoat, in the sacrificial system of Israel. The Lord directed Moses, saying: *"Then you will lead the two goats into my presence at the front of the sacred tent, where I will show you which goat will be sacrificed to me and which one will be sent into the desert to the demon Azazel. After you offer the first goat as a sacrifice for sin, the other one must be presented to me alive, before you send it into the desert to take away the sins of the people"* (Lev 16:7-10).

The scapegoat, which represented Satan -- once called Lucifer, the covering cherub -- was led away into the wilderness to his death. While Christ was sacrificed for all mankind, Satan ultimately bears the punishment for all the sins of all the redeemed, receiving the ultimate punishment of eternal destruction, as the sin of mankind (God's family) is passed from Christ (the sacrificial lamb) onto the head of Satan, the scapegoat (symbolically represented by the blood of the sacrificial lamb being poured on the head of the scapegoat, before it was led into the wilderness to its final destiny). The patriarch, Job, prophesied concerning this event, saying: *"He is driven from light into darkness and is banished from the world"* (Job 18:18). And Jude wrote: *"The angels who did not keep their positions of authority but abandoned their own home — these he has kept in darkness, bound with everlasting chains for judgment on the great Day"* ... *"They are wild waves of the sea, foaming up their shame; wandering stars, for whom blackest darkness has been reserved forever"* (Jude 6 & 13)

[3] Lucifer was created with profound musical talents and capabilities -- the sounds of percussion, stringed and wind instruments were created within him. This concept may have been understood by Ezekiel, to whom God gave the vision (Ezek 28:12-15), but has been difficult for his readers to understand. More recently, however, as God has revealed His mysteries, scientists have discovered that each of us has within us, a vast array of music.

Andrew Glazewski, in his book, "The Atom and The Octave" [1] presents considerable research into the correlations between phenomena such as plants, animals, crystals, atomic particle patterns, and the harmonics of music, concluded that "Atoms are harmonic resonators." In other words, the vibration of each atom is a kind of tiny musical note! Another researcher, Donald Andrews, has discovered that collections of atoms (or musical notes) in specific harmony with other atoms, forming what are commonly

12

referred to as molecules, are actually musical chords. "Continuing the expansion outward in size," Andrews says, "(these) molecules combine to form the various objects and forms of the world, each object and living being therefore being composed of a large number of molecules, or musical chords, which give the object or being its own individual and complex sound (or music). Hence the title of Andrews' new book, "The Symphony of Life" [2].

Similarly, each atomic vibration creates waves, which produce light and color. While the entire range of atomic vibrations is referred to in the science of physics as the spectrum of electromagnetic waves, the human eye can only perceive a very small portion of this spectrum. Beyond the range of visible light, are vibrations science refers to as ultraviolet light, X-rays, Gamma rays, etc. This spectrum of electromagnetism is referred to in modern physics in terms of 'octaves' due to the fact that these waves, in addition to producing sound, produce colors. The entire range of the known spectrum of magnetic waves encompasses seventy octaves of seven notes each. Interestingly, and no doubt through grand design, visible light occupies exactly one octave.

Molecular Biologists, relying on the research mentioned above, have converted the protein sequences in DNA into music. As reported in the Science Daily [3], May 16, 2007, "UCLA molecular biologists have turned protein sequences into original compositions of classical music. "We converted the sequence of proteins into music and can get an auditory signal for every protein," said Jeffery H. Miller, distinguished professor of microbiology, immunology and molecular genetics. ... "Every protein has a unique auditory signature because every protein has a unique sequence. ... "We assigned a chord to each amino acid," said Rie Takahashi, a UCLA research assistant and an award-winning, classically trained piano player. "We want to see if we can hear patterns within the music."

The result is that one can now go to various Internet sites and not only listen to DNA compositions, but submit one's own DNA sample, or one's unique genetic sequence and have it translated into music. (DNA) Deoxyribonucleic acid, is a nucleic acid that contains the genetic instructions used in the development and functioning of all known living organisms and some viruses. The main role of DNA molecules is the long-term storage of information. DNA is often compared to a set of blueprints or a recipe, or code, since it contains the instructions needed to construct other components of cells, such as proteins and RNA molecules. The DNA segments that carry this genetic information are called genes, but other DNA sequences have structural purposes, or are involved in regulating the use of this genetic information.

one helical turn = 3.4 nm

Sugar-phosphate backbone

Base

Hydrogen bonds

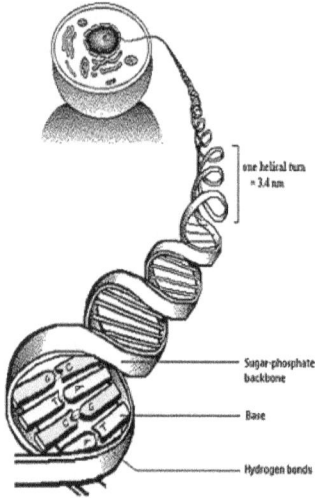

The structure of DNA is illustrated by a right handed double helix, with about 10 nucleotide pairs per helical turn. Each spiral strand, composed of a sugar phosphate backbone and attached bases, is connected to a complementary strand by hydrogen bonding (non-covalent) between paired bases of the proteins, adenine (A) with thymine (T) and guanine (G) with cytosine (C). Adenine and thymine are connected by two hydrogen bonds (non-covalent) while guanine and cytosine are connected by three.

Every living being, and object, is composed of DNA -- the same DNA, the only difference between one life form and another being in the arrangement of these four proteins and the spaces that lie between their groupings -- spaces that are filled with sound (i.e., music)! Since *"In Him (God) we live and move and have our being"* (Acts 17:28); and since *"God lives in us"* (1 Jn 4:12) -- in that *"We live in Him and He in us, because He has given us of His Spirit"* (1 Jn 4:13); God truly inhabits the praises of His people: *"Thou art holy, O thou that inhabitest the praises of Israel"* (Ps 22:3).

Only when one grasps this concept do Scriptures such as Psalm, 149 make sense. *"Praise the LORD! Sing to the LORD a new song, his praise in the assembly of the saints. Let Israel rejoice in their Maker; let the people of Zion be glad in their King. Let them praise his name with dancing and make music to him with tambourine and harp. For the LORD takes delight in his people; he crowns the humble with salvation. Let the saints rejoice in this honor and sing for joy on their beds. May the praise of God be in their mouths and a double-edged sword in their hands, to inflict vengeance on the nations and punishment on the peoples, to bind their kings with fetters, their nobles with shackles of iron, to carry out the sentence written against them. This is the glory of all his saints. Praise the LORD!"*

Solomon said: *"The crucible tests silver, the furnace tests gold, but a person is tested by his praise"* (Pro 27:21). When we are born-again [the Greek for this term literally meaning to be gened from above] (Jn 3:3 & 7; 1 Pe 1:23), our spirit or heart – the very core of our being: our DNA – sings a new song, carrying

14

out the mandate in Psalms 96:1; 98:1; 149:1; and Isaiah 42:10). Through our being gened from above (born-again) we can literally *"Pray in the spirit on all occasions"* (Eph 6:18); and "Pray without ceasing" (1 Th 5:17).

The Great Deception:
Lucifer, one of the covering cherubim and deputy, or director, over the heavenly choir (Ezek 28:14) knew a great deal about the structure of life. He knew that altering man's DNA would alter his ability to praise God. His position also gave him powerful influence over the other angels. He first used his influence to manipulate many of the angels to join in his rebellion -- those who were created as ministering spirits, created to minister to God and His family -- including His children: you and I! "To which of the angels did God ever say, *"Sit at my right hand until I make your enemies a footstool for your feet"? Are not all angels ministering spirits sent to serve those who will inherit salvation?"* (Heb 1:13-14).

Scripture is silent on the number of angels involved in this mutiny, however, since Satan is referred to as the great dragon, most theologians suggest that this mutiny involved a third of the angels, based on the words of John in Revelation. *"Then another sign appeared in heaven: an enormous red dragon with seven heads and ten horns and seven crowns on his heads. His tail swept a third of the stars out of the sky and flung them to the earth"* (Rev 12:3-4).

Lucifer, now called Satan, is one of the created angels -- not a member of the divinity. Job says: *"One day the angels came to present themselves before the LORD, and Satan also came with them. (Job 1:6-7 & 2:1).*

All of the angels -- including Lucifer -- were created by Christ Jesus. Paul wrote: *"He is the image of the invisible God, the firstborn over all creation. For by him all things were created: things in heaven and on earth, visible and invisible, whether thrones or powers or rulers or authorities; all things were created by him and for him"* (Col 1:15-16).

The angels' rebellion brought judgment on them: *"Then he will say to those on his left, 'Depart from me, you who are cursed, into the eternal fire prepared for the devil and his angels"* (Mt 25:41).

But Satan was not done with his fiendish scheme. Having diminished the number of angels committed to ministering to God's family, he next set out to manipulate man's DNA -- a scheme he actually achieved.

We read about this in Genesis 6. *"When men began to increase in number on the earth and daughters were born to them, the sons of God saw that the daughters of men were beautiful, and they married any of them they chose. Then the LORD said, "My Spirit will not contend with man forever, for he is mortal; his days will be a hundred and twenty years." The Nephilim were on the earth in those days — and also afterward — when the sons of God went to the daughters of men and had children by them. They were the heroes of old, men of renown"* (Gen 6:1-4). Proof of this event is preserved in skeletal remains, such as those exhumed in Syria (pictured right).

[4] Lucifer was anointed a covering cherub and commissioned to protect the hallowed mountain of God. Referencing the symbolism in the pattern revealed to Moses on Sinai, the pattern relied on in the construction of the tabernacle and its furnishings, the covering cherub guarded the mercy seat, or the throne of God. In addition to guarding God's throne, Lucifer was commissioned to protect the hallowed Mountain of God. This hallowed, or Holy Mountain, is elsewhere in Scripture referred to as Mount Zion, figuratively representing God's people (Is 60:14).

This spiritual symbolism of Mount Zion is carried forward into the New Testament, where it is referred to as God's spiritual kingdom, the heavenly Jerusalem (Heb 12:22; Rev 14:1). Peter refers to Christ as the Cornerstone [ruler] of Zion, saying: *"See, I lay a stone in Zion, a chosen and precious cornerstone, and the one who trusts in Him will never be put to shame"* (1 Peter 2:6).

[5] Lucifer walked among the fiery stones. This statement has little relevance without referring to the Book of Enoch, which was deleted from the cannon of Scripture by the Roman Catholic, College of Cardinals, during the Council of Nicea, in 325 AD. Following are brief exerts from the Book of Enoch which appear to be the foundation for the statement in Ezekiel, that Lucifer walked among the fiery stones: *"And the vision was shown to me thus: Behold, in the vision clouds invited me and a mist summoned me, and the course of the stars and the lightnings sped and hastened me, and the winds in the vision caused me to fly and lifted me upward, and bore me into heaven.*

"And I went in till I drew nigh to a wall which is built of crystals and surrounded by tongues of fire: and it began to affright me. And I went into the tongues of fire and drew nigh to a large house which was built of crystals: and the walls of the house were like a tessellated floor (made) of crystals, and its groundwork was of crystal. *Its ceiling was like the path of the stars and the lightnings, and between them were fiery cherubim, and their heaven was (clear as) water. A flaming fire surrounded the walls, and its portals blazed with fire. And I entered into that house, and it was hot as fire and cold as ice: there were no delights of life therein: fear covered me, and trembling got hold upon me.*

"And as I quaked and trembled, I fell upon my face. And I beheld a vision, And lo! there was a second house, greater than the former and the entire portal stood open before me, and it was built of flames of fire. **And in every respect it so excelled in splendor and magnificence and extent that I cannot describe to you its splendor and its extent. And its floor was of fire, and above it were lightnings and the path of the stars, and its ceiling also was flaming fire.**

"And I looked and saw therein a lofty throne: its appearance was as crystal, and the wheels thereof as the shining sun, and there was the vision of cherubim. And from underneath the throne came streams of flaming fire so that I could not look thereon. *And the Great Glory sat thereon, and His raiment shone more brightly than the sun and was whiter than any snow.* **None of the angels could enter and could behold His face by reason of the magnificence and glory and no flesh could behold Him.**

"The flaming fire was round about Him, and a great fire stood before Him, and none around could draw nigh Him: *ten thousand times ten thousand (stood) before Him, yet He needed no counselor. And the most holy ones who were nigh to Him did not leave by night nor depart from Him"* (En 14).

[6] **Lucifer's lifestyle was one of impeccable morality** -- perfect and without blemish -- until perverseness, or iniquity, appeared in him. What caused this perverseness? Ezekiel says: *"Your heart became proud on account of your beauty, and you corrupted your wisdom because of your splendor"* (Ezek 28:17).

Lucifer's Fall:

How could one, whose lifestyle was morally perfect, fall? What was this great wickedness found in Lucifer that caused his fall? And, what was its origin or cause? King Solomon answered these questions, saying: *"Avoiding evil is the highway of the upright; he who watches his step preserves his life. **Pride goes before destruction, and arrogance before failure.** Better to be humble among the poor than share the spoil with the proud"* (Prov 16:17-19).

The prophet, Ezekiel, confirmed that this was what resulted in Lucifer's fall. *"Through your widespread trade you were filled with violence, and you sinned. So I drove you in disgrace from the mount of God, and I expelled you, O guardian cherub, from among the fiery stones. **Your heart became proud on account of your beauty, and you corrupted your wisdom because of your splendor.** So I threw you to the earth; I made a spectacle of you before kings"* (Eze 28:16-17).

The prophet, Isaiah, also mentions Lucifer's fall, saying: *"How art thou fallen from heaven, O Lucifer, son of the morning! how art thou cut down to the ground, which didst weaken the nations! For thou hast said in thine heart, I will ascend into heaven, I will exalt my throne above the stars of God: I will sit also upon the mount of the congregation, in the sides of the north. I will ascend above the heights of the clouds; I will be like the most High. Yet thou shalt be brought down to hell, to the sides of the pit. "They that see thee shall narrowly look upon thee, and consider thee, saying, Is this the man that made the earth to tremble, that did shake kingdoms; That made the world as a wilderness, and destroyed the cities thereof; that opened not the house of his prisoners?"* (Is 14:12-17).

Notice the words of God expressed through the prophet, Ezekiel: *"**I expelled you, O guardian cherub**, from among the fiery stones. ... Your heart became proud on account of your beauty, and you corrupted your wisdom because of your splendor. **So I threw you to the earth**; I made a spectacle of you before kings"* (Ezek 28:16-17).

Satan's Scheme for Revenge:

Satan -- previously known as Lucifer -- had walked among the fiery stones surrounding God's throne. He was one of the covering cherubs, guarding the throne. He was one of the highest, if not the highest, created beings. As such, he knew a great deal about God's plans and purposes. There is little doubt that he knew of God's plan to create children (Adam and Eve), for, although he had been expelled from God's presence, he lurked in the Garden of Eden, near the Tree of Life, waiting to get even with God!

Personal Application:

In what area, or areas of your life have you allowed pride to manifest, clouding your values and obscuring your virtues:

[ ] Physical Beauty or Physique
[ ] Sexual Prowess
[ ] Talents and/or capabilities
[ ] Achievements
[ ] Possessions
[ ] Preoccupation with self
[ ] Feeling Better than Others
[ ] Contempt of others
[ ] Overreaction to Criticism
[ ] Egocentricity
[ ] Jealousy
[ ] Grasping after another person's position
[ ] Keeping up with the Jones'

[ ] Other _____

[ ] Other _____

[ ] Other _____

Of all the things God says that He hates, Pride tops the list. *"These six things the Lord hates, yes, seven are an abomination to Him: A proud look, a lying tongue, hands that shed innocent blood, a heart that devises wicked plans, feet that are swift in running to evil, a false witness who speaks lies, and one who sows discord among brethren"* (Prov. 6:16-19).

Repentance:
"God resists the proud but He gives grace to the humble" (James 4:6). Ask the Lord to show you this sin in your heart. Pray for meekness and humility of mind and heart as did David, when he prayed: *"Search me, O God, and know my heart; test me and know my anxious thoughts. See if there is any offensive way in me, and lead me in the way everlasting"* (Ps 139:23-24).

Ministry:
Confess your weakness in this area and ask others to pray for you. *"Confess to one another therefore your faults (your slips, your false steps, your offenses, your sins) and pray [also] for one another, that you may be healed and restored [to a spiritual tone of mind and heart]. The earnest (heartfelt, continued) prayer of a righteous man makes tremendous power available [dynamic in its working]"* (James 5:16 AMP).

[Throughout Scripture -- including the Apocryphal books, Satan and his angels, while seeking to be restored to the heavenly choir, never once confessed their sins or asked for forgiveness.]

God's Promised Healing:
"The fear of the LORD teaches a man wisdom, and humility comes before honor" (Prov 15:33); *"Humility and the fear of the LORD bring wealth and honor and life"* (Prov 22:4).

Discipleship Guidance:
"Therefore, as God's chosen people, holy and dearly loved, clothe yourselves with compassion, kindness, humility, gentleness and patience" (Col 3:12-13).

Footnotes:
[1] The Atom and The Octave: A 21st. Century Search for Synthesis, Andrew Glazewski:
1. http://www.atomandoctave.co.uk/EZ/atom/atom/page04.php
2. The Symphony of Life, Donald Andrews, Unity Books, 1986.
3. The Science Daily, http://www.sciencedaily.com/
4. Your DNA Song, http://www.yourdnasong.com

Chapter Two ~ War On Planet Earth

Lurking near the Tree of Life, Satan watched and listened as Adam named each animal, seeking longingly a mate of his own. He could, no doubt, sense Adam's desire. Then, Adam beheld Eve and said: *"At last! This is bone from my bones and flesh from my flesh. She is to be called Woman [Hebrew: ishah], because she was taken out of Man [Hebrew: ish]"* (Gen 2:23 CLB). When Satan heard Adam's expression of pleasure, he knew that if he could deceive Adam's mate, Eve, he would have won Adam's unwilling compliance to his scheme.

Waiting patiently, until he caught Eve alone near the Tree of The Knowledge of Good and Evil, *"[Satan] The serpent, (who) was more crafty than any wild animal which Adonai, God, had made, said to the woman, "Did God really say, 'You are not to eat from any tree in the garden'?" The woman answered the serpent, "We may eat from the fruit of the trees of the garden, but about the fruit of the tree in the middle of the garden God said, 'You are neither to eat from it nor touch it, or you will die.'"* (Gen 3:1-2).

God had indeed warned Adam and Eve not to eat from the Tree of the Knowledge of Good and Evil. *"The Lord God enjoined (instructed) mankind concerning the garden: 'eat liberally from any and all the trees, but never eat from the tree of pleasures and prosperity: adversity, affliction and calamity. The consequences declared for living a life eating from the 'tree' of pleasures and prosperity: adversity, affliction and calamity (for a season); is most assuredly death"* (Gen 2:16-17).

Cunning Deception:

"The serpent said to the woman, "It is not true that you will surely die; because God knows that on the day you eat from it, your eyes will be opened, and you will be like God, knowing good and evil." When the woman saw that the tree was good for food, that it had a pleasing appearance and that the tree was desirable for making one wise, she took some of its fruit and ate. She also gave some to her husband, who was with her; and he ate" (Gen 3:1-6). A clearer translation might of verse 4 reads: *"Serpent declared to the woman: "never worthy of death! [Most] assuredly, in the season (dimension) you consume from (it), your senses will be expanded, enabling you to see everything!*

"And," Satan continued, *" a great thing will follow; you will be able to correctly discern, like Supreme beings (gods), all moral adversity, affliction, calamity, wickedness and wretchedness."*

What a cunning temptation. Satan assured the woman that by eating of the fruit of the tree in question, she and the man would experience something great -- their senses would be expanded. Eating from the tree would, Satan claimed, enable them to see all moral issues, and the effects, there of, with proper discernment, enabling them to make wise decisions! Grasping the import of the temptation, it is perhaps, somewhat easier to understand the woman's response. A better translation of her response reads: *"And when the woman beheld that the tree was certainly exceedingly beautiful to behold, and inasmuch (and therefore) surely good -- an eatable provision -- a delectable thing, greatly desired to make one intelligent, enhance one's understanding and give wisdom,*

22

she picked some and carried it away, consuming it and sharing it with her husband accompanying her, and he consumed (devoured) it" (vs. 5-6).

Tragic Transmutation:
As a result of their eating of this fruit, their senses were expanded. The King James version reads: *"Then the eyes of both of them were opened, and they realized they were naked; so they sewed fig leaves together and made coverings for themselves"* (Gen 3:7). A clearer translation reads: *"Their senses were expanded and they beheld pleasure and prosperity: displeasure and affliction; and they recognized (discerned) their nudity. Therefore,they dressed, putting together something of foreign origin for the purpose of armoring, or girding (themselves)."*

Adam's and Eve's initial awareness of the gravity of their disobedience was that they discerned their nudity. Their sense of nudity was, however, far more profound than one might experience from being unclothed. After all, no one except themselves, and on occasion God -- Who knew made them and knew all about them -- was in the garden. They had been clothed in God's Shekinah Glory, which when they sinned, had departed, leaving them disembodied spirits. [For a detailed analysis of this passage, see Chapter 5, "Man's Rebellion and Fall," in "Mysteries of the Bible -- Adam to Abram: The Primeval Era, Potter, James V. and Paula M., Advocare Publishing CA, 2009.]

As a result of this profound loss, they covered themselves with some foreign substance, until God in his love, covered them with skin -- flesh and blood -- (Gen 3:21). As loving as this was, their new bodies of flesh and blood merely reminded them of their profound loss. And, while most of us have lost sight of the origin of man's plight, we all *"groan, earnestly desiring to be clothed upon with our house which is from heaven"* (2 Cor 5:2). Or, as the Greek implies: *"we intensively crave possession -- to be supplied with our habitation (residence) that originates out of the abode of God, as a wrapper (an outer garment)."*

THE INNER VOID

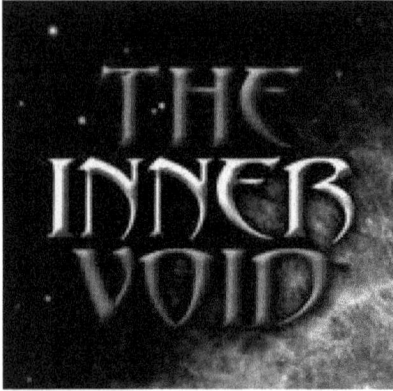

Even worse, far worse, than the loss of the Shekiniah Glory that had clothed them, they felt a profound sense of emptiness within. They recognized the cause: God's Spirit -- the Indwelling Holy Spirit -- had withdrawn from them. One of the Apocryphal books sadly omitted from the cannon -- the Wisdom of Solomon -- makes mention of this.

The opening words of this ancient book deal specifically with this loss. *"Love justice, you who rule the earth; Be mindful of the Lord in goodness, and seek him in singleness of heart. For he is found by those who do not test him, and reveals himself to those who have full trust in him. Devious thoughts cut men off from God, and the divine power, when made trial of, exposes the foolish.*

*"For **Wisdom** will not enter a fraudulent mind, nor make **her** home in a body mortgaged to sin. The **Holy Spirit, that divine tutor**, will fly from cunning stratagem; **she** will withdraw from unintelligent thoughts and will take umbrage at the approach of injustice.*

*"**Wisdom** is a **benevolent spirit** and **she** will not hold a blasphemer immune from his own utterances; because God is a witness of his thoughts, the real guardian of his mind, who hears every word. For the **spirit of the Lord fills the world**, and that which holds all things together has knowledge of all articulate sound. No one, therefore, who celebrates injustice will escape notice, nor will justice the accuser pass him by"* (WS 1:1-8).

Satan, having accomplished his deceptive scheme, Adam and Eve were divested of God's Shekinah Glory and Holy Spirit's indwelling companionship. They were subsequently clothed in skin, like the animals, but were filled with agony over their plight. God's presence upon and within them had departed: they felt all alone and very vulnerable.

Warfare Rules of Engagement:
This tragic event transferred the spiritual warfare from the heavens to the earth. The battle that had begun in heaven between Michael and his angels, and Satan (Lucifer) now involved mankind. In fact, mankind -- God's children -- had now become the focal point of the battle: a battle for man's souls.

One would think that Michael and his angels, who had defeated Satan and his angels in the heavenly realm (Rev 12:7-8), would have no difficulty defeating them on earth. However, there was another factor that must now be considered. Mankind had dominion over the earth, and everything on it (Gen 1:28; Ps 8:3-8).

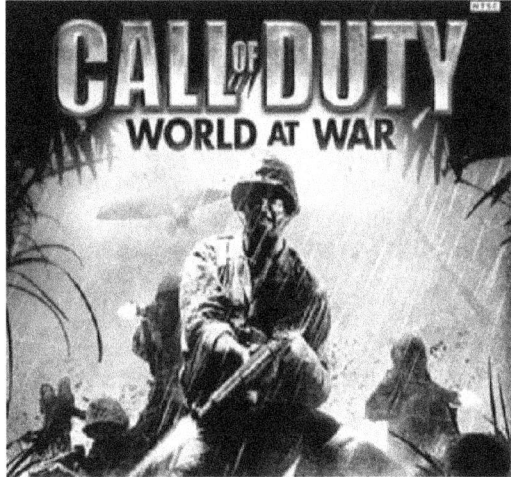

God, in his love, and sense of justice and righteousness, would not overrule man in his rightful domain. Thus, Michael and his angels would be available to help men who called upon God, while Satan and his angels would gladly assist those who denied God's authority in their lives, or rebelled against Him.

To a large degree, the outcome of the spiritual battle on earth rested with mankind, and who he gave spiritual allegiance to -- either The Lord God Almighty, or Satan. The Serpent or Dragon [once called Lucifer, the Light-bearer] (Rev 12:9), expelled from heaven and cast upon the earth, now went out to deceive the whole earth (Rev 20:8), and *"prowls around like a roaring lion, looking for someone to devour"* (1 Pe 5:8).

Combat Casualty Care:
Every battlefield has demanded a casualty care and field surgery unit, and this conflict of the cosmos -- now being fought on planet earth -- is no exception. This battlefield (Planet Earth) has been blessed with an unequaled casualty care unit that is capable of healing every spiritual, psychological and physical wound. This 'casualty care unit' is the 'church', a word derived from the Greek word, 'ekklesia', which refers to an assembly, or popular meeting, referring particularly to a congregation of saints.

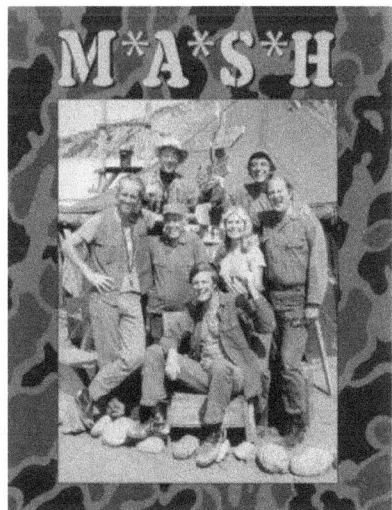

The Greek word, ekklesia, correlates with the Hebrew word, 'qahal' we find in the Old Testament – a word that also refers to an assembly, congregation or multitude.

The Origin of God's Church: We read of the church's origin in Job 38:7, when at the establishment of the foundation of the earth, "the morning stars sang together and all the angels shouted for joy." The assembly of the saints is next mentioned in our present Cannon of Scripture (the Bible) after God had delivered the nation of Israel from Egypt, and gave Moses instructions concerning their covenant responsibilities. In Exodus, we read: "On the first day hold a sacred assembly, and another one on the seventh day" (Ex 12:16). In Leviticus, the assembly was commanded to gather at the Tent of the Meeting [the Tabernacle] (Lev 8:3-4); and soon thereafter, they were instructed to assemble on a weekly basis.

"The LORD said to Moses, "Speak to the Israelites and say to them: 'These are my appointed feasts, the appointed feasts of the LORD , which you are to proclaim as sacred assemblies. There are six days when you may work, but the seventh day is a Sabbath of rest, a day of sacred assembly. You are not to do any work; wherever you live, it is a Sabbath to the LORD" (Lev 23:1-3). It was at the Tabernacle, when Israel had assembled, that the Lord appeared to speak to them and give them directions (i.e., Num 16:19 & 42).

Extra-canonical Witness:
No where, perhaps, is there a more descriptive account of the eternal nature of God's church than in the book, The Shepherd of Hermas, - one of the books eliminated from the cannon. Written between 120-140 AD, identifies the author as Hermas, the Shepherd, the brother of Pius I, Bishop of Rome. Tertullian implies that Pope Callixtus I quoted from it as an authority. Clement of Alexandria constantly quoted with reverence from this work, as did Irenaeus, Origen and other early church fathers.

Some biblical scholars suggest that Hermas – pictured right in an ancient wood cutting – is the man named in Paul's letter to the Romans (Rom 16:14). The Book of Hermas contains a number of visions, two of which are very pertinent. The first depicts the church as a woman, which is consistent with other scriptural references, in both Old and New Testaments. In vision one Hermas says: *"Moreover, brethren, it was revealed to me, as I was sleeping, by a very considerate young man, saying to me, What did you think of that old woman from whom you received the book; who is she? I answered, A Sybil."*

[A sybil was a female diviner of the future.] *"You are mistaken, he said, she is not. I replied, Who is she then, sir? He answered me,* **It is the Church of God. And I said to him, Why then does she appear old? He said, She is therefore an old woman, because she was the first of all the creation, and the world was made for her"** (Vision 2:31-33).

Following this, Hermas concludes this vision, with a short encounter with 'the old woman' that serves as a bridge to his next vision. *"After this I saw a vision in my own house: the old woman whom I had seen before came to me and asked me whether I had yet delivered her book to the elders of the church. I answered that I had not yet. She replied, You have done well, for I have certain words more to tell you. But when I shall have finished all the words, they will be clearly understood by the elect. And you will write two books, and send one to Clement and one to Grapte. Clement will send it to the foreign cities, because it is permitted to him so to do, but Grapte will admonish the widows and orphans. But you will read it in this city with the elders of the church"* (vs 34-37).

In Vision 3, the development of the church and the spiritual warfare Christians would be engaged in, are introduced through the metaphor of the construction of a building -- a great tower -- the church triumphant. Once again, this symbolism is consistent with those Scriptures included in the accepted cannon. [For example, the apostle, Paul, says: *"Husbands, love your wives, just as* **Christ loved the church and gave himself up for her to make her holy, cleansing her by the washing with water through the**

word and to present her to himself as a radiant church, *without stain or wrinkle or any other blemish, but holy and blameless"* (Eph 5:25-28).]

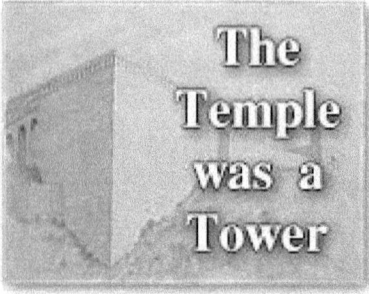
The Temple was a Tower

Hermas says: *"I began to entreat her for the Lord's sake that she would show me the vision she had promised. Then she again took me by the hand and lifted me up, and made me sit upon the seat on the left side, and holding up a certain bright wand, said to me, See that great thing? I replied, Lady I see nothing. She answered, Do you not see opposite you a great tower with bright square stones built upon the water? For the tower was built upon a square by these six young men who came with her.*

Lively Stones From God's Quarry:
"But many thousands of other men brought stones; some drew them out of the deep, others carried them from the ground, and gave them to the six young men. And they took them and built. As for those stones that were pulled out of the deep, they put them all into the building, for they were polished, and their squares exactly corresponded to one another that one was joined to the other so that there was no space to be seen where they joined, so much so that the whole tower appeared to be built as if it were of one stone.

"But as for the other stones that were taken off from the ground, some of them they rejected, others they fitted into the building. As for those that were rejected, some they cut out and cast at a distance from the tower, but many others of them lay round about the tower, which they made no use of in the building. For some of these were rough, others had clefts in them, others were white and round, not proper for the building of the tower.

"But I saw the other stones cast afar off from the tower and falling into the highway, and yet not continuing in the way, but were rolled from the way into a desert place. Others I saw falling into the fire and burning; others fell near the water, yet could not roll themselves into it, though very desirous to fall into the water. And when she had showed me these things she would have departed, but I said to her, Lady, what does it profit me to see these things and not understand what they mean? She answered and said to me, You are very shrewd to desire to know those things which relate to the tower.

Yes, I said, Lady, so that I may declare them to the brethren, and they may rejoice, and hearing these things may glorify God with great glory. Then she said, Many indeed will hear them, and when they will have heard them, some will rejoice, and others weep. And yet even these, if they will repent, will rejoice too" (Vision 3:22-35).

"*As for the tower which you see built, it is myself, namely the Church, which appeared to you both now and before. Therefore ask what you will concerning the tower, and I will reveal it to you, so that you may rejoice with the saints. I said to her, Lady, because you have thought me once worthy to receive from you the revelation of all these things, declare them to me. She answered me, Whatever is fit to be revealed to you will be revealed; only let your heart be with the Lord, and do not doubt whatever you will see.*

"*I asked her, Lady, why is the tower built upon the water? She replied, I said before to you that you were very wise to inquire diligently concerning the building, therefore you will find the truth. Hear therefore why the tower is built upon the water: because your life is and will be saved by water. For it [baptism] is founded by the word of the almighty and honorable name, and is supported by the invisible power and virtue of God. (vs. 38-41). "And I answering, said to her, These things are very admirable, but Lady, who are those six men that build? She said, They are the angels of God who were first appointed, and to whom the Lord has delivered all his creatures, to frame and build them up, and to rule over them. For by these the building of the tower will be finished.*"

[Compare Paul's writing, where he states: "*You are no more strangers and foreigners, but fellow citizens with the saints and the household of God; being built upon the foundation of the apostles and prophets, Jesus Christ himself being the chief corner [stone]; In whom all the building fitly framed together groweth unto an holy temple in the Lord: In whom ye also are builded together for an habitation of God through the Spirit*" (Eph 2:21).]

Then, continuing, Hermas, continuing to quote the lady in his vision, writes: "*And who are the rest who bring them stones? They also are the holy angels of the Lord, but the others are more excellent than these. When the whole building of the tower will be finished, they will all feast together beside the tower, and will glorify God because the structure of the tower is finished*" (vs 45-46). [This allegory is consistent with both Isaiah's and Peter's writings. Isaiah says, "*Listen to me, you who pursue righteousness and who seek the LORD: Look to the rock from which you were cut and to the quarry from which you were hewn*" (Is 51:1).

© Ritmeyer Archaeological Design

Peter, employing this same allegory, wrote: *"Ye also, as lively stones, are built up a spiritual house, an holy priesthood, to offer up spiritual sacrifices, acceptable to God by Jesus Christ"* (1 Peter 2:5). Jesus also employed this same metaphor, telling Peter: *"And I tell you that you are Peter [Petros, a building block or paving stone] but upon this rock [Petra, a stone mountain, or firm foundation] I will build my church, that the gates of Hades will not overcome it"* (Mt 16:18).]

"I asked her, saying, I would know the condition of the stones, and the meaning of them, what it is? (vs. 47) ... **The square and white stones which agree exactly in their joints, are the apostles, and bishops, and doctors, and ministers, who through the mercy of God have come in, and governed, and taught and ministered holy and modestly to the elect of God**, *both those who have fallen asleep and those who yet remain, who have always agreed with them, and have had peace within themselves, and have heard each other. For this reason their joints exactly meet together in the building of the tower.*

*"***They which are dug out of the deep and put into the building, and whose joints agree with the other stones that are already built, are those who have suffered for the sake of the Lord's name and are already fallen asleep***. And what are the other stones, Lady, that are brought from the earth? I would know, what are they? She answered,* **They that lie upon the ground and are not polished, are those which God has approved because they have walked in the law of the Lord and directed their ways in his commandments**. *They that are brought and put in the building of the tower are young in faith and*

the faithful. And these are admonished by the angels to do well because iniquity is not found in them" (vs. 52-57).

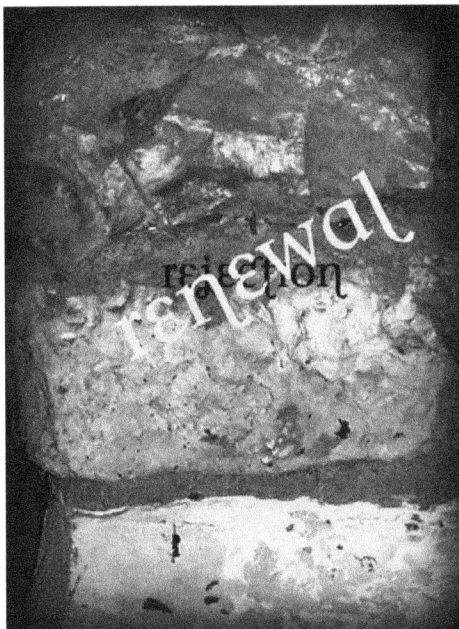

"But who are those whom they rejected and laid beside the tower? They are such as have sinned and are willing to repent; for this reason they are not cast far from the tower, because they will be useful for the building, if they will repent. *They therefore that are yet to repent, if they will repent, will become strong in the faith; that is, if they repent now, while the tower is building. For if the building will be finished, then there will be no place for them to be put in, but they will be rejected, for he only has this privilege who will now be put into the tower"* (vs. 58-60).

But would you know who **they are that were cut out, and cast afar off from the tower**? *Lady, I said, I desire it.* **They are the children of iniquity, who believed only in hypocrisy,** *but departed not from their evil ways; for this they will not be saved, because* **they are not of any use in the building by reason of their sins.** *Therefore they are cut out and cast afar off, because of the anger of the Lord, and because they have provoked him to anger against them.*

"As for the great number of **other stones you have seen placed about the tower but not put into the buildings, those that are rugged are they who have known the truth, but have not continued in it,** *nor been joined to the saints, and therefore are of no use.* **Those that have clefts in them are they that keep up discord in their hearts against each other and live not in peace,** *who are friendly when present with their brethren, but as soon as they are departed from one another, their wickedness still continues in their hearts: these are the clefts which are seen in those stones.* **Those that are maimed and short are they who indeed have believed but still are in great measure full of wickedness**; *this is the reason they are maimed and not whole"* (vs 61-66).

*"But what are **the white and round stones**, Lady, and which are not suitable for the building of the tower? ... **They are such as have faith indeed, but have the riches of this present world besides**. When therefore any tribulations arise, for the sake of their riches and traffic, they deny the Lord. I answering, said to her, When therefore will they be profitable to the Lord? She said, When their riches in which they take delight will be cut away, then they will be profitable to the Lord for his building. As a round stone's bulk cannot be made square unless it be cut away and part discarded, so they who are rich in this world, unless their riches be pared off, cannot be made profitable to the Lord. Learn this from your own experience, for you also once were one of those stones: when you were rich you were unprofitable, but now you are profitable and fit for the life which you have undertaken"* (vs 67-72).

*"**As for the rest of the stones which you saw cast afar off from the tower, and running in the way, and tumbled out of the way into desert places, they are such as have believed indeed, but through their doubting have forsaken the true way**, thinking they could find a better. But they wander and are miserable, going into desolate ways.*

*"Then for **those stones which fell into the fire and were burned, they are those who have finally departed from the living God**; nor does it ever come into their hearts to repent, by reason of the affection which they bear to their lusts and wickedness which they commit. And what are **the rest which fell by the water, and could not roll into the water? They are such as have heard the word and were willing to be baptized in the name of the Lord, but considering the great holiness which the truth requires, have withdrawn themselves and walked again after their wicked lusts**"* (vs 73-76).

This ends Hermas' allegory of the church triumphant. However, the entire book is well worth reading. The remainder of Vision 3 deals specifically with the spiritual battle for man's souls and concludes with these words: *"Whoever therefore will serve these and hold fast to their works, he will have his dwelling in the tower with the saints of God. Then I asked her concerning the times, whether the end was now at hand.*

"But she cried out with a loud voice, saying, O foolish man! Do you not see the tower yet being built? When therefore the tower will be finished, and built, it will have an end; and indeed it will soon be accomplished" (vs. 91-93).

These visions of Hermas, together with references from our cannon of Scriptures, depict the spiritual battle taking place on the earth. We are all -- by the fact that we are humans -- part of this great conflict in the cosmos, that has come to earth.

The question then, is not whether we will participate in this battle, but rather, whether we will be among the victors, or the victims.

Personal Application:
Reflecting on Hermas' vision of the construction of the tower -- the church triumphant -- which type or types of stones describe your present spiritual condition?

[ ] A perfectly square, white stone that agrees exactly with other similar stones fitting together through the mercy of God, who is given to teach and minister to others?
[ ] A stone rescued from the deep (lost in sin), that has responded to life in such a manner that you are polished and fit perfectly into the Body of Christ, enjoying harmony with others?
[ ] A stone that is still rough, that is around the church, but not really a functional part of it?
[ ] A stone that has cracks in it, making it unsuitable in building the church?
[ ] A stone that fell in the highway of life, not continuing in his/her spiritual growth?
[ ] A stone that has distanced itself from the church and is now in a desert place?
[ ] A stone that has fallen into the fire, which will burn unless rescued?
[ ] A stone that wishes to get lost in the water (the multitudes in the world)?
[ ] A stone that is well fitted but needs to be polished in order to be useful in the church?
[ ] A stone that is young in the faith, but free from iniquity?
[ ] A stone lying next to the tower, rejected because of sin, but willing to repent?
[ ] A stone that was rejected, but has repented of his/her sin and has become strong in the faith and ready to fit into the church?
[ ] A stone that was cut to fit, but because of iniquity and hypocrisy, has been cast from the church?

[ ] A stone that was cut to fit, but because of iniquity and hypocrisy, has been cast from the church?

[ ] A stone that is rugged, who has known the truth, but have not continued to walk therein, becoming unprofitable?

[ ] A stone that is marred with cracks due to the discord in their heart toward others in the church?

[ ] A stone that is two-faced: friendly with others face to face, but hostile toward them behind their backs?

[ ] A stone that is maimed and short, who has believed but who still holds a great deal of wickedness in his/her heart?

[ ] A stone that is white and round, self-righteous, but unwilling to fit into the church?

[ ] A stone that has faith but is caught up in the riches of this present world?

[ ] A stone that once professed faith but when troubles arose, turned away from, or denied the Lord?

[ ] A stone, who running from the church in a difficult time, tumbled into a dry and desert place?

[ ] A stone who once believed, but through doubting has forsaken the way, thinking they might find a better path?

[ ] A stone who has fallen into the fire and was burnt, departing from the living God?

[ ] A stone who shuns God due to the lust in their heart and the wickedness they commit?

[ ] A stone who heard the Word of the Lord, but considering the commitment and holiness required, withdrew from God.

[ ] One who has failed to see that our struggle is not against flesh and blood?

[ ] Other _____?

The Remedy:

Regardless of the type of stone you perceive yourself to be, you need merely repent and follow the counsel of Isaiah, who wrote: *"Listen to me, you who pursue righteousness and who seek the LORD: Look to the rock from which you were cut and to the quarry from which you were hewn"* (Is 51:1). ... *"The Lord says: "I have no pleasure in the death of the wicked; but that the wicked turn from his way and live: turn ye, turn ye from your evil ways; for why oh why will ye die?* (Ezek 33:11).

Return, thou backsliding [ones], saith the LORD ; and I will not cause mine anger to fall upon you: for I am merciful, saith the LORD , and I will not keep anger for ever. Only acknowledge thine iniquity, that thou hast transgressed against the Lord thy God, and hast scattered thy ways to the strangers under every green tree, and ye have not obeyed my voice, saith the Lord. Turn, O backsliding children, saith the Lord; for I am married unto you: and I will take you one of a city, and two of a family, and I will bring you to Zion: And I will give you pastors according to mine heart, which shall feed you with knowledge and understanding" (Jer 3:12-15). ... *"Return faithless people and I will heal your backsliding"* (vs 22). *"I will save them from all their sinful backsliding and I will cleanse them. They will be my people, and I will be their God"* (Eze 37:23).

Ministry:

Do you feel worthless? Do you think you are too old to be useful in the church? Or do you, perhaps, think you have drifted too far from God, or have become so hardhearted or indifferent, that there is no hope? Listen to the words of the prophet, Jeremiah:

"This is the word that came to Jeremiah from the Lord: "Go down to the potter's house, and there I will give you my message." So I went down to the potter's house, and I saw him working at the wheel. But the pot he was shaping from the clay was marred in his hands; so the potter formed it into another pot, shaping it as seemed best to him. Then the word of the Lord came to me: "O house of Israel, can I not do with you as this potter does?" declares the Lord . "Like clay in the hand of the potter, so are you in my hand?" (Jer 18:1-6).

Surrender your life anew to God, placing your life in His hands, like clay in the potter's hand, trusting Him to heal you, anoint and equip you for service.

May the God of peace, who through the blood of the eternal covenant brought back from the dead our Lord Jesus, that great Shepherd of the sheep, equip you with everything good for doing his will, and may he work in you what is pleasing to him, through Jesus Christ, to whom be glory for ever and ever. Amen" (Heb 13:20-21).

Footnotes:

[1] Wisdom of Solomon, Doubleday & Co. 1979; also available online at: http://www.earlyjewishwritings.com/wisdom.html

[2] The Shepherd Hermas, The book, The Shepherd Hermas, can be accessed online, or downloaded, at:
http://ministries.tliquest.net/theology/apocryphas/nt/hermvis.htm

Chapter Three ~ Introducing the Enemy

James V. Potter @ 17 - 1954

After entering the US Navy, during the Korean Conflict in 1954, I (Doc) along with the other recruits, were exposed to hours of movies and lectures designed to acquaint us with the enemy. Before joining the battle, we needed to know what our enemy looked like -- to be able to distinguish them from our own troops -- to avoid what has been called 'friendlyfire'. We needed to understand their culture, know how they think, know their strengths, their weaknesses, and idiosyncrasies; and know how to act should we be attacked or taken captive.

As Christians engaged in spiritual warfare – a battle that all humans are engaged in, whether we are aware of it or not – we have as much, if not a greater, need to comprehend these features of our enemy, enabling us to differentiate between our enemy and our fellow warriors. This is what the apostle Paul addressed in his letter to the Ephesians. To find answers to these questions and concerns, let's first review what we have discovered thus far:

In Chapter 1, we learned that Lucifer was not only one of the Cherubim, he was a covering Cherub, Standard-bearer of the Sacred Colors, Director of the Heavenly Choir, and Director over the angels who were to be Ministering Spirits to mankind. We saw that he became prideful of his beauty and position, conceived a scheme to elevate his throne (position) above Jehovah (Yeshua, or Christ). To accomplish his scheme, he tricked one-third of the angels into joining his rebellion. The result was that both Lucifer and the angels who joined him, were expelled from the Garden of

Expelled from the Garden of God – the seventh dimension – Lucifer and the angels who aligned themselves with him, were cast into the earth– the sixth dimension.

In Chapter 2, we discovered that after his fall, Lucifer -- now Satan -- deceived Adam and Eve, contributing to their rebellion and fall. As a result of their rebellion, Adam and Eve were divested of God's Shekinah Glory which their spirit had been enveloped in; and were deprived of the indwelling influence of Holy Spirit.

The result – they were dark, their spirit empty and they were sorely afraid. God, in His loving kindness, enveloped them in skin (flesh and bones); but due to their rebellion, they too were expelled from the Garden of Eden -- Into the sixth dimension.

Outside the Garden of Eden -- the seventh dimension -- everything was far different. They no longer had access to the tree of life and they were subject to the elements. The ground was cursed because of their sin and produced thorns and thistles. Amongst these they had to till the ground by the sweat of their brow, to grow their own food (Gen 3:17-19) Their visibility was now limited -- the moon giving only one-seventh of its light and the sun now being no brighter than the sun had been (Is 30:26).

Having achieved his initial objective, Satan now set about to alter man's DNA, by engaging some of the Watchers -- angels commissioned to watch over man -- to interbreed with the daughters of men, thereby corrupting their genetics. Their offspring, the Nephilim, were giants who taught mankind every form of evil, after which they turned against man and, being carnivorous, became cannibals and consumed man. This first infestation of Nephilim were destroyed in Noah's flood, but as predicted (Gen 6:4), the Watchers returned and once again infested the earth with giants.

It was these giants, the Nephilim, the Raphiam, the Zamzummiams, and similar races, who the descendants of Abram -- the Israelites -- met when they crossed the Jordan River to possess Canaan. David and his men killed the last of the giants in Canaan (2 Sam 21:22), but the damage had been done -- giants now covered the earth, corrupting the seed of man.

Even worse than the Nephilim's and their ilk's corruption of the seed of man; upon their their spirits – evil spirits – now roamed the earth, soon earning themselves the name, 'demons' (Is 8:19-22). Unlike the seed of man, once dead, they had no hope of a resurrection. The Prophet Isaiah, declared: *"They are now dead, they live no more; those departed spirits do not rise"* (Is 26:14).

The apostle John makes it very clear that the fallen angels were cast out of the Garden of Eden into the earth at the same time: *"And there was war in heaven: Michael and his angels fought against the dragon; and the dragon fought and his angels and prevailed not; neither was their place found any more in heaven. And the great dragon was cast out, that old serpent, called the Devil, and Satan, which deceiveth the whole world: he was cast out into [not onto] the earth, and his angels were cast out with him"* (Rev 12:7-9).

The Greek text says *[eblee'thee eis tee'n gee'n]*, which correctly transliterated, declares: *"he was thrust **into** the earth or ground."* Satan, leader of the angelic rebellion, was not only cast out of Heaven **onto** the earth, he was according to the original Greek text, cast **into** the earth -- **imprisoned in the abyss**. Moreover, the rest of this verse in the Greek says *[kai hoi angeloi autou met autou eblee'theesan]*, which correctly transliterated, states: *"and those angels of his, together with him were **thrust"**,* suggesting that both Satan and his rebellious conspirators were thrust into, rather than cast onto, the earth – imprisoned in the abyss until the end-time.

In the end-time, Satan -- the fallen angel (star) will be given the key to the abyss and allowed to open it (Rev 9:1-5). At that time, beings ascend out of the abyss who are permitted to torment all men who have not received the seal of God [Holy Spirit] (Rev 9:4; 1 Cor 1:22). The church speaks a great deal about doing battle with evil angels, yet the Bible says very little about them. Although, having been cast out of heaven and imprisoned in the earth, they are still under God's authority and serve at His bidding. For example, when Pharaoh refused to let the children of Israel leave Egypt, God sent destroying angels to strike down all of Egypt's first born.

"He unleashed against them his hot anger, his wrath, indignation and hostility — a band of destroying angels. He prepared a path for his anger; he did not spare them from death but gave them over to the plague. He struck down all the firstborn of Egypt, the first fruits of manhood in the tents of Ham" (Ps 78:49-51).

On another occasion, *"God sent an evil spirit between Abimelech and the men of Shechem; and the men of Shechem dealt treacherously with Abimelech, that the cruelty done to the threescore and ten sons of Jerubbaal might come, and their blood be laid upon Abimelech their brother, which slew them; and upon the men of Shechem, which aided him in the killing of his brethren"* (Jdg 9:23-24). In another instance, *"God sent an angel unto Jerusalem to destroy it: and as he was destroying, the Lord beheld, and he repented him of the evil, and said to the angel that destroyed, It is enough, stay now thine hand"* (1 Ch 21:15). God also sent a destroying angel to deal with the Assyrians. *"And the Lord sent an angel who annihilated all the fighting men and the leaders in the camp of the Assyrian king"* (2 Ch 32:31).

In contrast to these limited instances of evil or destroying angels being mentioned in Scripture, there are literally hundreds of references to God's holy angels who have been sent by God to interact with man. For example, angels have been sent:
- To convey a message or charge from God,
- To man to minister to one of His servants, or children in need,
- To provide guidance,
- To protect, guard, rescue and deliver His children,
- To go ahead of his children who he is sending into an area to prepare the way,
- To drive His children's enemies out of the land He gives them,
- To intervene with man on God's behalf,
- To encourage,
- To bring God's blessings,
- To open wombs at God's direction,
- To do battle on behalf of God's children,
- To minister a healing touch,
- To serve as a mediator between God's children,
- To pursue and even destroy the enemies of God's people,
- To control the behavior of animals for His children,
- To open prison doors to set His missionaries free, and
- To give those in ministry specific direction and guidance.

There are of course many other reasons God has sent, and continues to send, His holy angels to communicate with man, or act on his behalf – with or without man's request or knowledge.

Recognizing Our Enemy:
This brings to bear a vital question. If Satan and his angels are imprisoned in the abyss, and God's holy angels -- directed by Michael -- make war on our behalf, and at our request to God, who are we fighting? And, what is this thing we call 'spiritual warfare' all about? The apostle Paul answered these questions saying: *"Finally, be strong in the Lord and in his mighty power. Put on the full armor of God so that you can take your stand against the devil's schemes. For our struggle is not against flesh and blood, but against the rulers, against the authorities, against the powers of this dark world and against the spiritual forces of evil in the heavenly realms"* (Eph 6:10-13).

Paul's answer to these questions would have been perfectly clear to his first and second century readers. However, it has lost some of its clarity to us living in the twenty-first century. To help us clear up the confusion, we turn again to the Greek text. A transliteration of Ephesians 6:10 reads:

"Henceforth (or in the remaining time), increase your strength being in Christ and in the might of his dominion (the church). Clothe yourself with the full armor of God, so that it might be possible for you to stand (maintain a position) against the trickery of the seducer (devil). Because we never wrestle (struggle) against blood and flesh; contrariwise, it is against the magistrates (principalities), against the superhuman potentates, against the rulers of this obscurity (darkness or unseen), against the ethereal (non-carnal) malicious wickedness in the celestial."

In other words, Paul clarified that our struggle is not against flesh and blood but against those magistrates (principalities), superhuman potentates, and the rulers of obscurity -- the unseen -- who being non-carnal inhabit the celestial (the heavenly). Notice that Paul does not include the fallen angels.

41

Why? They are imprisoned in the earth (abyss), until the end-times. Our struggle is not against flesh and blood (other humans), nor is it against the fallen angels who are confined in the abyss. **Our battle is solely against the principalities, powers and rulers of obscurity (the unseen), who inhabit the air.**

Put more clearly, our battle is with the demons. Demons, the disembodied spirits of the Nephilim -- the offspring of the Watchers. Demons -- also referred to as evil spirits (Lk 4:33) -- are never mentioned in Scripture until after the Watchers had interbred with the daughters of women, and their offspring, the Nephilim, were destroyed by a great flood in Noah's day. Demons are ethereal (non-carnal) unseen – to humans – (obscure) creatures of malicious wickedness who operate in the air.

In detailed consistency with Paul's descriptive reference of them and their kingdom, demons:
- Are organized militarily in legions (Mk 5:15),
- Are ruled by a prince (Mt 12:24; Mk 3:22),
- Have superhuman strength (Lk 8),
- Perform miraculous signs (Rev 16:14),
- Are malicious, teaching man ungodly things (1 TI 4:1),
- Inhabit places (Rev 18:2),
- Inhabit animals (Mt 8:31-33; Lk 8:30-35),
- Inhabit people (Lk 4:14).
- Cause illness (Mt 9:33
- Cause insanity (Mt 17:15-18; Lk 4:33),
- Cause impairments such as being mute (Lk 11:14).

The people living during Paul's lifetime, and in the centuries before Christ came to earth, sought to appease demons by sacrificing to them and worshipping them (Dt 32:17; Ps 106:37). The worship of demons seems to have begun, or at least to have become organized, with the founding of the mystery religions, under Nimrod and his queen, Semarimis, in ancient Babylon.

When God destroyed the Tower of Babel, He confused men's languages, and subsequently divided the earth (Gen 10:25; 1 Ch 1:19). This resulted in linguistically coherent groups of Babylonians migrating to various places, taking with them the mystery religion – the worship of demons. So pervasive was this cunning deception that even the Patriarch, Jacob, inculcated it in his thought processes. Being gravely ill in his old age, and knowing his time on earth was short, he called together his twelve sons to bless them.

In his last blessing over his sons, Jacob associated each one with one of the twelve constellations represented by the Zodiac. One of the groups who migrated from Babylon became known as the Greeks. The Greeks carried demon worship to a completely new level, developing a complete pantheon of gods. Over time, the Greeks came to worship not scores, nor just hundreds, but literally thousands of demons, whom they considered gods -- each being assigned over specific territories, specific animals, plants, etc.

Scattered among the nations, as a consequence for their waywardness, many of the Israelites were taken captive by the Babylonians and Assyrians, and later sold by them to the Greeks (Joel 3:8). While in servitude to the Greeks, the nation of Greece was conquered by the Romans, who being demon-worshippers themselves, conveniently embraced the Greek Pantheon of gods, giving them Latin names. The Olympian deities embraced by Greeks and Romans alike -- whom many of the Israelites had also come to venerate -- included the following:

- **Aphrodite** - goddess of love, lust, beauty, seduction and hedonistic pleasure.

- **Apollo** - god of music, plagues and healing, prophecy, poetry, and archery.

- **Ares** - god of war, bloodlust, violence, manly courage, and civil order.

- **Artemis** - virgin goddess of the hunt, of wilderness, wild animals, childbirth, and plagues.

- **Athena** - virgin goddess of wisdom, warfare, strategy, heroic endeavors, handicrafts and reason.

- **Demeter** - goddess of fertility, agriculture, horticulture, grain and harvest.

- **Dionysus** - god of wine, parties, festivals, madness, drunkenness, lewdness and pleasure.

- **Hades** - king of the underworld and god of death and dying, of the dead, and the hidden wealth of the earth.

- **Hephaestus** - crippled god of fire, metalworking, stone masonry, sculpture, and volcanism.

- **Hera** - queen of heaven, goddess of marriage, women, childbirth, inheritance, kings and empires.

- **Hermes** - god of travel, messengers, trade, thievery, cunning wiles, language, diplomacy, athletics, and animal husbandry.

- **Hestia -** virgin goddess of the hearth, home and cooking.

- **Poseidon** - god of the sea, rivers, floods, droughts, earthquakes and horses.

•**Zeus** - king of the gods, ruler of Mount Olympus and god of the sky, weather thunder, law, order and fate. When Paul penned his letter to the Ephesians (c 60 AD), the principle city of Ephesus, boasted a pagan temple that had been dedicated to the Roman goddess Diana – (Artemis/ Cybele) in Greek.

When Paul penned this epistle, it was but three short years until Rome would overthrow Jerusalem, tear down the temple and erect on the temple mound, a temple to their god Jupiter (Greek Zeus).

Israel had, by the time Christ came to earth, become so corrupt her people were offering sacrifices to demons and burning incense on the high places and under the green trees, set aside to honor them (2 Ki 16:4; Jer 2:20; 3:6; Eze 6:13). They knew that many of their problems stemmed from the demons they worshipped, yet they felt hopeless, believing they must continue to worship them and sacrifice to them lest something worse befall them. Then, when Jesus came among them and began ministering to them, they had hope.

Jesus Exercised Authority Over Demons:

Jesus expelled demons from the insane, from the violent, from the deaf mutes, from those with leprosy, from prostitutes, from those inflicted by demons with various illnesses -- in fact, it seemed that all illnesses were associated with demon oppression. Jesus not only delivered people of virtually every kind of demon oppression, infestation and possession, he even raised the dead! The demons were afraid of him, as they themselves expressed. *When he arrived at the other side in the region of the Gadarenes, two demon-possessed men coming from the tombs met him.*

They were so violent that no one could pass that way. "What do you want with us, Son of God?" they shouted. "Have you come here to torture us before the appointed time?" Some distance from them a large herd of pigs was feeding. The demons begged Jesus, "If you drive us out, send us into the herd of pigs" (Mt 8:28-31).

Christ's Apostles Given Authority Over Demons:

Moreover, the demons were not only afraid of Jesus, they were afraid of those whom he commissioned to carry on his ministry. *"When Jesus had called the Twelve together, **he gave them power and authority to drive out all demons and to cure diseases**, and he sent them out to preach the kingdom of God and to heal the sick"* (Luke 9:1-3).

Authority Extended to Christ's Disciples:

*"**After this the Lord appointed seventy-two others and sent them two by two** ahead of him to every town and place where he was about to go. He told them, "The harvest is plentiful, but the workers are few. Ask the Lord of the harvest, therefore, to send out workers into his harvest field. Go! I am sending you out like lambs among wolves. Do not take a purse or bag or sandals; and do not greet anyone on the road. "When you enter a house, first say, ' Peace to this house.' ... Heal the sick who are there and tell them, 'The kingdom of God is near you.' ... **The seventy-two returned with joy and said, "Lord, even the demons submit to us in your name"*** (Luke 10:1-17).

Jesus taught both his apostles and disciples to carry out the ministry of reconciliation (2 Cor 5:19) -- reconciling humanity back to God, a principle part of which involved expelling demons and healing the sick. Then, after personally demonstrating the ministry of reconciliation for three and one-half years, long enough to train up a group of dedicated teachers who could replicate his ministry, thereby multiplying (building-up) the church, he commissioned them. *"Then Jesus came to them and said, "All authority in heaven and on earth has been given to me. Therefore go and make disciples of all nations, baptizing them in the name of the Father and of the Son and of the Holy Spirit, and teaching them to obey everything I have commanded you. And surely I am with you always, to the very end of the age"* (Mt 28:18-20).

Jesus even assured them of success. *"I tell you the truth, anyone who has faith in me will do what I have been doing. He will do even greater things than these, because I am going to the Father. And I will do whatever you ask in my name, so that the Son may bring glory to the Father. You may ask me for anything in my name, and I will do it"* (John 14:12-14).

Mark's record of this event is a bit different and worth including here for the sake of the comment that follows: *"He said to them, "Go into all the world and preach the good news to all creation. Whoever believes and is baptized will be saved, but whoever does not believe will be condemned. And these signs will accompany those who believe: In my name they will drive out demons; they will speak in new tongues; they will pick up snakes with their hands; and when they drink deadly poison, it will not hurt them at all; they will place their hands on sick people, and they will get well. After the Lord Jesus had spoken to them, he was taken up into heaven and he sat at the right hand of God. **Then the disciples went out and preached everywhere, and the Lord worked with them and confirmed his word by the signs that accompanied it"*** (Mark 16:15-20).

A Shift in the Balance of Power:
Something dramatic had changed in the conflict of the cosmos. Christ's apostles and disciples, and their disciples -- empowered by being in Christ and Christ in them -- accomplished the same acts that Christ had. What effected this difference?
- They were appointed and anointed by Christ,
- They were indwelled by Holy Spirit,
- They were specifically given authority over demons (Lk 9:1),
- They had the ability to request legions of angels from Father God as needed (Mt 26:53),

Michael and his angels (God's holy angels) -- ministering angels to God's family -- the family of man -- are still available in whatever numbers necessary, to help us wage a winning war in the spiritual realm: our war against the demons! We need only resist the demons and they will flee (Jas 4:7); resist him and stand firm in the faith (1 Per 5:9).

46

"And the God of all grace (spiritual enabling), Who called you to His eternal glory in Christ -- after you have suffered a little while -- will himself restore you and make you strong, firm and steadfast" (vs 10).

Christ gave us authority and dominion over the demons -- not over the fallen angels, nor over other humans. The angels -- both holy and unholy -- appear to serve solely at God's direction. Jesus, while in the flesh, indicated that he would need to ask the Father to send him legions of angels (Mt 26:53) and *"Michael, the archangel, when contending with the devil disputing over the body of Moses, durst not bring a railing accusation against him, but said 'The Lord rebuke thee'"* (Jude 9). Where then, is the basis for the tradition within the church, that we are to exercise authority over them?

Testimonies of a Winning Stratagem:
This ministry of reconciliation (reconciling humanity to God and godliness) seemingly continued unabated throughout the first and on into the third or fourth century AD. The Book of Acts records a number of healings and spiritual deliverance involving the apostles (Acts 4:9-14 & 22; 5:16; 8:7; 14:9; 28:8). Of particular interest, because of its specific note concerning the apostles expelling demons is the story in Acts 5:

Acts of the Apostles
"Meanwhile, through the emissaries (ambassadors) [presumably those the apostles had trained] many signs and miracles continued to be done among the people. United in mind and purpose, the believers met in Shlomo's [Solomon's] Colonnade; and no one else dared to join them. Nevertheless, the people continued to regard them highly; and throngs of believers were added to the Lord, both men and women. They went so far as to bring the sick into the streets and lay them on mattresses and stretchers, so that at least Kefa's [Peter's] shadow might fall on them as he passed by. Crowds also gathered from the towns around Yerushalayim [Jerusalem], bringing the sick and those afflicted with unclean spirits; and every one of them was healed" (Acts 5:12-16).

Testimony of James
The Book of James encourages those needing the ministry of healing and deliverance to look to the church, promising them healing, forgiveness and deliverance. *"Is someone among you ill? He should call for the elders of the congregation. They will pray for him and rub olive oil on him in the name of the Lord. The prayer offered with trust will heal the one who is ill — the Lord will restore his health; and if he has committed sins, he will be .*

Forgiven, Therefore, openly acknowledge your sins to one another, and pray for each other, so that you may be healed. The prayer of a righteous person is powerful and effective" (Jas 5:14-17).

Additional Testimony of Apostles:
The Books of Acts and James are certainly not the only testimony to the continued ministry of healing and deliverance. In the Acts of Thomas, a collection of writings not included in our present-day cannon of Scripture, yet attested to by early church fathers, include numerous accounts of deliverance, healings and raising the dead.

The original composition of these writings is believed to be dated in the first half of the 3d century, slightly later than the Acts of the Apostles that were first used by Irenaeus late in the 2nd century, and the Acts of Peter, John, Paul, Andrew, Philip, Thecla, the disciple of Paul, Hermas, a disciple of Paul, and others, which are attested to have been written during the late the 2d century. Some sections, particularly the originally independent Hymn of the Pearl, presuppose conditions in the Parthian period, which ended with the establishment of the Sassanian Empire in 226 CE Some form of the work was clearly in circulation by the end of the 4th century when testimonies begin since Epiphanius (Anac. 47.1 and 0.1.5) records its use by Encratites, Augustine, the Manicheans, the Faustum, etc.

Testimony of Early Church Fathers:
There is substantial evidence that spiritual deliverance, or the expelling of demons or evil spirits was routinely practiced in the early church. Following are but a few references:
1. Irenaeus Against Heresies, Book II, 32:4 (190 AD) - *"For some (Christians do certainly and truly drive out devils, so that those who have thus been cleansed from evil spirits frequently both believe and join themselves to the church."*
2. Justin Martyr, Second Apology, Ch. 8 (153 AD) - This apology was addressed to the Roman Senate. *"And they (demons), having been shut up in eternal fire, shall suffer their just punishment and penalty. For if they are even now overthrown by men through the Name of Jesus Christ, this is an intimation of the punishment in eternal fire which is to be inflicted on themselves and those who serve them."*
3. Second Apology, Ch. 6 - *"And now you (Roman Senate) can learn this from what is under your own observation. For numberless demoniacs throughout the whole world, and in your city, many of our Christian men exorcising them in the Name of Jesus Christ, who was crucified under Pontius Pilate, have healed*

and do heal,rendering helpless and driving the demons out of men, though they could not be cured by all the other exorcists, and those who used incantations and drugs."

[Note that deliverance included healing from various diseases.]

1. Justin Martyr, Dialogue With Trypho, a Jew, Ch. 30 (150 AD) *"For we call Him (Jesus) Helper and Redeemer, the power of whose name even the demons do fear; and at this day, when they are exorcised in the Name of Jesus Christ, they are overcome."* Ch. 76 *"And now we, who believe on our Lord Jesus, who was crucified under Pontius Pilate, when we exorcise all demons and evil spirits, have them subjected to us.*

2. Tatian, Address of Tatian to the Greeks, Ch. 16 (160 AD) *"Sometimes they themselves (demons) disturb the habit of the body by a tempest of folly; but, being smitten by the Word of God, they depart in terror, and the sick man is healed."* [Once again, spiritual exorcism included healing from disease and illness.]

3. Theophilus, Theophilus to Autolycus, Book II. 8 (160-180 AD) Theophilus is refuting the false teachings of Homer and Hesiod who were famous Greek poets. *"...And this clearly appears from the fact, that even to this day the demonized are sometimes exorcised in the Name of the living and true God and these spirits of error themselves confess that they are demons who also formerly inspired these writers (Homer and Hesiod)."*

4. Tertullian, Apology, Ch. 23 (197 AD) *"Let a person be brought before your tribunals; who is plainly under demonic possession. The wicked spirit, bidden to speak by a follower of Christ, will as readily make the truthful confession that he is a demon, as elsewhere he has falsely asserted that he is a god."*

5. Tertullian, To Scapula, Ch. 4 *"The clerk of one of the courts who was liable to be thrown upon the ground by an evil spirit, was set free from his affliction (by Christians); as was also the relative of another, and the little boy of a third. How many men of rank (to say nothing of common people) have been delivered from demons, and healed of diseases?"*

6. Minucius Felix, The Octavious of Minucius Felix (210 AD) *"A great many, even some of your own people, know all those things that the demons themselves confess concerning themselves, as often as they are driven by us (Christians) from bodies by the torments of our words and by the fires of our prayer."* (The Ante-Nicene Fathers, Vol. IV, p. 190).

7. Minucius Felix, The Octavious of Minucius Felix (210 AD) *"A great many, even some of your own people, know all those things that the demons themselves confess concerning themselves, as often as they are driven by us (Christians) from bodies by the torments of our words and by the fires of our prayer."* (The Ante-Nicene Fathers, Vol. IV, p. 190).

8. Lactentius, The Divine Institutes, Book II, 16 (250-320 AD) - *"But they (demons) fear the righteous, that is, the worshipers of God, adjured by whose name they depart from the bodies (of people); for being lashed by the Christians' words, they not only confess to be demons, but even utter their own names."* Book V., 22, *"For He (Holy Spirit) employs the tongue of one man for wisdom; the soul of another He enlightens by prophecy, to another He gives power to drive away demons..."*

9. The Divine Institutes, Book V, 22 *"For these (demons), as long as there is peace among the people of God, flee from the righteous, and fear them; and when they seize upon the bodies of men, and house their souls, they are adjured by the Christians, and at the Name of the true God are put to flight. For when the demons hear of this name they tremble, cry out, and assert that they are branded and beaten; and being asked who they are, whence they are come, and how they have insinuated themselves into a man, confess it. Thus, being tortured and excruciated by the power of the Divine Name, they come out of the man."*

There are numerous other references to healings, spiritual deliverances, even the dead being raised, throughout the writings of the early church fathers. Yet, as one reads their treatises, one cannot help but notice that over time, there were fewer and fewer references to exorcisms and divine healings. From the writing of these early church fathers, several things are apparent:

1. Spiritual deliverance in the early church involved deliverance -- not only from the more overt manifestations of **demonic possession and oppression**, but incorporated the less obvious: healing from **addictions** and **illness**.

2. Spiritual deliverance and divine healings were the norm in the first century apostolic age.

3. The manifestation of such spiritual power was one of the greatest **testimonies of the gospel** expressed by the early church.

4. Spiritual deliverance and divine healings did not stop upon the death of Christ's apostles, nor upon the death of their direct disciples, as claimed by many Protestant mainstream theologians.

Diminished Faith Within the Church:

Given such a powerful model -- through Jesus and his disciples -- what has happened to our faith? Within the body of Christ today, only twenty-six percent (26%) of Christians believe in faith healing, expelling demons and raising the dead. Even fewer practice this ministry of reconciliation so that the world may know.

The apostle Paul seems to have anticipated our present condition, and our question. He said:

"But mark this: There will be terrible times in the last days. People will be lovers of themselves, lovers of money, boastful, proud, abusive, disobedient to their parents, ungrateful, unholy, without love, unforgiving, slanderous, without self-control, brutal, not lovers of the good, treacherous, rash, conceited, lovers of pleasure

pagan goddesses

Sun-goddesses breast-feeding their sun-god babies.

Notice the "Halo" or "Nimbus" around their heads - to signify the sun-god mother and child.

rather than lovers of God— having a form of godliness but denying its power. Have nothing to do with them. They are the kind who worm their way into homes and gain control over weak-willed women, who are loaded down with sins and are swayed by all kinds of evil desires, always learning but never able to acknowledge the truth" (2 Tim 3:1-7).

Dancing With Demons:

What happened? The answer is simple: it was the church's subservience to the influence of Greek paganism. From historian, La Dues' writings, it is easy to connect the fact that **changes within the doctrines of the church were believed 'necessary'** to resolve the political conflict between Christianity and Hellenism in the **4th century AD.** Consider, for example, the pagan and symbolism that has pervaded Christianity, as depicted in the following paragraphs:

If you look carefully, you will see that baby Jesus and Mary, are depicted in the same manner as Tammuz and his mother, Semiramis, Queen of ancient Babylon. Semiramis and Nimrod were the founders of the ancient mystery religions that pervaded Hellenistic thought -- the same mystery religions that John said all the world would wonder after (Rev 17:5). Once again, the apostle, Paul, seemingly having been given prophetic insight, wrote:

"The Spirit clearly says that in later times some will abandon the faith and follow deceiving spirits and things taught by demons. Such teachings come through hypocritical liars, whose consciences have been seared as with a hot iron" (1 Tim 4:1-2).

Other counterfeit teachings from paganism that have crept into the church include the following. Check each one of these teachings that you presently practice, or have in the past, believed in, relied on, and or practiced.

[ ] A fixed order of service in most churches that has become so rigid in many that there is no room for a move of the Spirit.
[ ] A belief that within each of us -- at the core -- is righteousness and truth, often referred to as the 'Christ consciousness' within.
[ ] A belief in magic to influence others, the world, etc.
[ ] Belief in and reliance on astrology.
[ ] Belief in and reliance on numerology.
[ ] Belief in the power of crystals and/or pyramids.
[ ] Belief in the healing power of birth stones or other stones.
[ ] Belief in spirit channeling.
[ ] Belief in the power of Totems, animal or other.
[ ] Belief that colors have specific spiritual powers.
[ ] Belief in Tarot cards or other fortune telling routines.
[ ] Belief in crystal ball fortune telling.
[ ] Belief in palm-reading to determine one's future.
[ ] Belief in the mystic/spiritual powers of certain herbs.
[ ] Belief in and reliance on the Zodiac.
[ ] Belief in Chakra orientation of life and healing through the Chakra with crystals, meditation, etc.
[ ] Belief in and practice of transcendental meditation.
[ ] Belief in the healing power of moonstones.
[ ] Belief in the healing power of gemstones.
[ ] Belief in and/or practice of Yantra.
[ ] Belief in casting spells.

[ ] Belief in and use of the Ouija Board.

[ ] Belief in and reliance on tea-reading.

[ ] Belief in psychic readings.

[ ] Belief in and reliance on Karma.

[ ] Belief in Reincarnation.

[ ] Belief in the reading of auras.

[ ] Belief in personal transformation – i.e., the ability to heal one's self.

[ ] Belief in transmigration – having been an animal in past lifetimes, or the possibility of becoming one in future lifetimes.

[ ] Belief in and reliance on spiritual mediums or channelers.

[ ] Belief in. practice of, and reliance on clairvoyance.

[ ] Belief in, practice of, and reliance on extra sensory perceptions (ESP).

[ ] Belief in and reliance on certain rituals.

[ ] Belief that finding a horseshoe brings good luck.

[ ] Belief that breaking a mirror brings bad luck.

[ ] Belief that garlic protects one from evil spirits.

[ ] Belief in other superstitions.

[ ] Belief in and practice of Eastern Philosophy.

[ ] Belief in and practice of any form or white or black magic.

[ ] Believing if one's behavior causes no one else harm, there is no victim, making the behavior permissible.

[ ] Believing that the Divine One has made Itself manifest through different Deities in different places and at different times in earth's history.

[ ] Believing that God is in everyone and everything, which is Pantheism.

[ ] Believing that Christianity is not the only avenue to salvation.

[ ] Believing in astral projection and/or astral travel, also referred to as Ekankar.

[ ] Believing that finding a coin heads up brings good luck.

[ ] Building elaborate churches - first century Christians worshipped in homes. Only after Constantine (c320 AD) did the church turn its focus from using its resources to spread the gospel to that of elaborate building churches and temples.

[ ] Celebrating Christmas as sacred - the 25th of December was the birthday of Tammuz, the 'savior' of the mystery religions. When Christ was born, the shepherds were out on the hills surrounding Bethlehem, tending their sheep -- highly unlikely on December 25.

[ ] Celebrating Easter as sacred - Easter is named after Ishtar, the goddess of springtime, a title given Semiramis after her death.

[ ] Celebrating Halloween as having spiritual significance -- honors a Druid ritual of offering sacrifices to the dead.

[ ] Chasing Easter eggs - that honor the great 'mystic egg' that was, according to the mystery religion of Babylon, the origin of planet earth.

[ ] Crossing your fingers to avoid bad luck.

[ ] Hero worship of one's pastor, teacher, an actor, etc.

[ ] Lust (over-desire) of the flesh, the eye and the pride of life (our property and possessions)

[ ] Making decisions based on a throw of the dice.

[ ] Making decisions based on drawing straws.

[ ] Making decisions based on casting lots.

[ ] Making decisions based on drawing high/low cards.

[ ] Member of the Rosicrucians.

[ ] Necromancy - worshiping, talking to, or loving the dead.

[ ] Playing "Christian" rock and blues music that absorb, rather than emit energy, that evoke sensual rather than spiritual response, do little to edify believers. A broken meter in treble, played over an insistently regular beat with gradually increasing rapidity is capable of producing the identical disintegrating and almost hysterical effect on an organism ... any psychiatrist knows that it is precisely this two-directional pull of conflicting drives of emotions that is helping to fill our mental hospitals with broken wrecks of humanity.

[ ] Practice of fortune telling, or manipulation which are witchcraft.

[ ] Practice of Masonry or any other secret society where vows are taken, other than vows to God.

[ ] Practice of witchcraft.

[ ] Reliance on mystic energy for guidance and/or healing.

[ ] Relying on your own intellect, emotions, or beliefs, in place of God, for guidance in your life.

[ ] Relying on a rabbit's foot, or four leaf clover for good luck.

[ ] Worship of any icon, or believing that they have the power to bring good luck or prevent bad luck.

[ ] Worship of, or relying on messages from, angels.

[ ] Worshipping, anything or anyone other than God.

54

Ministry:
Belief in, reliance on, or practice of, any of the things mentioned above, or similar things, will prevent one from being victorious in their Christian walk or effective in any aspect of ministry, including spiritual warfare.

It is most effective when dealing with these to do so with another committed Christian, carrying out the instructions of James, who wrote: *"Openly acknowledge your sins to one another, and pray for each other, so that you may be healed. The prayer of a righteous person is powerful and effective"* (James 5:16-17 CJB).

In prayer, confess to the Lord, and the other person ministering to you, and then renounce, each of the beliefs or practices you marked, along with any similar belief or practice that Holy Spirit brings to your remembrance. After renouncing each one, ask Father God for His forgiveness, and ask Holy Spirit – Who indwells your spirit – to alert you should you begin to slip back into any of these practices.

If you have taught any of these practices to your children, or others, confess the error of your ways, and ask for their forgiveness. Satan, and the demons assigned to you, will come to remind you of your past involvement in these things, and accuse you of unrighteousness. Their effort is to cause you to question God's forgiveness and your salvation. But, we may be assured that, *"If we confess our sins, he is faithful and just and will forgive us our sins and purify us from all unrighteousness"* (1 John 1:9-10).

Knowing that our sins are forgiven, we may *"draw near to God with a sincere heart in full assurance of faith, having our hearts sprinkled to cleanse us from a guilty conscience"* (Heb 10:22); and *"approach God's throne of grace with confidence, so that we may receive mercy and find grace to help us in our time of need"* (Heb 4:16).

Having this confidence, we will be assured that, *"There is no longer any condemnation for those united in spirit-to-Spirit union with the Messiah Yeshua"* (Rom 8:1).

Chapter Four ~ Equipping for Battle

"Put on the full armor of God so that you can take your stand against the devil's schemes. For our struggle is not against flesh and blood, but against the rulers, against the authorities, against the powers of this dark world and against the spiritual forces of evil in the heavenly realms" (Eph 6:10-12).

"Therefore put on the full armor of God, so that when the day of evil comes, you may be able to stand your ground, and after you have done everything, to stand.

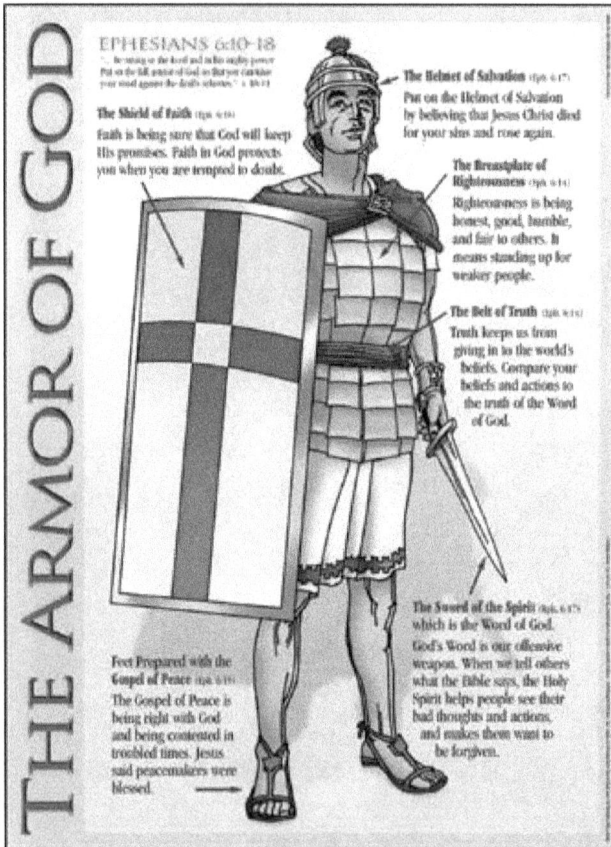

"Stand firm then, with the belt of truth buckled around your waist, with the breastplate of righteousness in place, and with your feet fitted with the readiness that comes from the gospel of peace. In addition to all this, take up the shield of faith, with which you can extinguish all the flaming arrows of the evil one. Take the helmet of salvation and the sword of the Spirit, which is the word of God.

"And pray in the Spirit on all occasions with all kinds of prayers and requests. With this in mind, be alert and always keep on praying for all the saints" (Eph 6:10-13).

Induction into the Army:

After entering the military, there are many things one must master during boot camp. These include how to wear the approved uniform, and how to use the approved weaponry. Unlike the military, the church does not require new converts to attend boot camp. However, new Christians -- being novices in the Word -- should not strike out on their own, but should rely on the more experienced -- the captains, admirals, and sergeants of the faith -- to teach them the art of warfare. It is also desirable, but not mandatory, that new converts complete a discipleship program.

The Armor of God:

God's armor ensures victory because it is far more than a protective covering. It is the very life of Jesus Christ Himself. Paul, in his letter to the Roman Christians, wrote: *"Put on the armor of light,* **clothe yourselves with the Lord Jesus Christ***"* (Rom 13:12-14) When we are *in* Christ, He becomes our hiding place, our shelter in the time of storm -- just as He was to David (Ps 61:4; 91. Hidden in Him, you are assured of victory -- His victory -- for He not only covers you as a shield, He also fills you with His life. He said: *"I am the vine; you are the branches,* **if a man abides in Me and I in him, he will bear much fruit; apart from me you can do nothing***"* (Jn 15:5). ... *"If you remain in me, and my words remain in you, ask whatever you wish, and it will be given you"* (Jn 15:7).

Living within the safety of the armor of God means oneness with Jesus. Being one in Him, we can expect to share His struggles as well as His victories and peace. Remember, God has promised us victory in the midst of trials, not immunity from pain. So *"***do not be surprised at the painful trial** *you are suffering, as though something strange were happening to you, but* **rejoice that you participate in the sufferings of Christ***..."* (1 Pe 4:12-13). Christian heroes who have been tortured for their faith testify to the supernatural strength -- even joy -- that enabled them to endure unthinkable pain.

They affirm with Paul, that -- *"in all these things we are more than conquerors through him who loved us. ... For I am persuaded that neither death nor life, neither angels nor demons, neither the present nor the future, nor any power. ... will be able to separate me from the love of God that is in Christ Jesus our Lord"* (Rom 8:37-39). This wonderful truth has become a reality to all who believe, take up their cross, and follow Jesus. When you put on His armor, His life envelops you, keeping you safe, close to Himself, free to be His precious friend and trusted companion. **So,** *"***put on Christ***"* (Gal 3:27); for **He is your victory**!

Putting on God's Armor:

Truth: Living in Christ begins with learning about, validating, and trusting in each part of the armor. The first component of the armor is truth -- God's revelation, through the written word and the indwelling Holy Spirit, of all that God has done for us, and all that He promises to do for us in the days ahead. His enduring truth is written in the Bible, revealed by the Holy Spirit, and realized through our life in Jesus Christ. It pierces every worldly distortion, deception, and compromise. When you study, memorize, and live your life according to God's truth, it enables you to see the world from a different perspective -- God's perspective. Putting on this first piece of God's armor involves feeding on His truth through daily Bible reading, thereby making it literally, a part of yourself.

Armor Component	Characteristics	Key Scriptures
Belt of Truth	The **Truth** of God	Dt 4:39; Ps 23:1; 18:1-3
Breastplate of Righteousness	**Righteousness** of Christ in You	Ps 100:3; Rom 3:23-24; 6:23; Gal 2:20-21; Phil 3:8-10
Sandals of Peace	Inner **Peace** and Security	Rom 5:1; Eph 2:14; Jn 14:27; 16:33, 20:21
Shield of Faith	Living in **Faith**	Rom 4:18-21; Heb 11:1; 1 Pe 1:6-7
Helmet of Salvation	**Salvatio**n in Christ	Ps 16 & 23; Heb 1:3-6; 2 Co 4:16-18; 1 Th 4:17; 1 Jn 3:103
Sword of the Spirit (God's Word)	Countering Spiritual Deception through God's Word	Heb 4:12; Mt 4:2-11; 1Pe 3:15; Ps 119:110-112

Put on the "full armor of God" -- and **enjoy your daily walk and eternal love-relationship in Christ Jesus**. Thank Him for His Word, and what He is revealing to you as you submit your petitions and search His Word.

By wearing the special protection God offers us through His armor, we will be able to stand firm against Satan's strategies. Remember, the armor of God is not some magic shield you can casually slip on in order to be safe anywhere you want to go. When you go somewhere you shouldn't, or if you disobey God, you are essentially "taking off" the breastplate of righteousness. You're never safe, if you go somewhere Jesus wouldn't want you to go, or do something you know is against his will.

Know the Scriptures that validate your prayers so that your words and faith are grounded in the authority of the Bible. (Some of those verses are listed in the chart above.) Then, pray through each piece of armor as you put it on.

Weapons of Spiritual Warfare:

1) **Prayer --** Paul's instructions for putting on the whole armor of God, are followed by the following directive -- to pray -- which is the first, and most important weapon in the arsenal of the spiritual warrior. *"Pray in the Spirit on all occasions with all kinds of prayers and requests. With this in mind, be alert and always keep on praying for all the saints"* (Eph 6:13).

The scope of prayer -- i.e., the different types of prayer, and their application -- is such that we have devoted the entire next chapter to this primal spiritual warfare weapon.

Demonstrating the power of prayer, Jesus, praying for Simon Peter, said: *"Simon, Simon, Satan has asked to sift you as wheat. But I have prayed for you, Simon, that your faith may not fail. And when you have turned back, strengthen your brothers"* (Lk 22:31-32). Satan, whose obsession is to *"steal, kill and destroy"* (Jn 10:10), will endeavor to sift every one of us -- particularly those engaged in spiritual warfare against his purposes. The apostle, Paul, recognizing this, said:

*"**I (Paul) urge that supplications, prayers, intercessions, and thanksgiving be made for all men, for kings and all who are in high positions,** that we may lead a quite and peaceable life, godly and respectful in every way. This is good and acceptable in the sight of God our Savior, who desires all men be saved and come to the knowledge and truth"* (1 Ti 2:1-4).

Intercessors in the New Testament, are to the New Covenant Church, what the Watchmen on the Walls, were to Israel in the Old Covenant. Of them, it was said: *"I have posted watchmen on your walls, O Jerusalem; **they will never be silent day or night**. You who call on the Lord, give yourselves no rest, and give him no rest till he establishes Jerusalem and makes her the praise of the earth"* (Is 62:6-7).

We, of the New Covenant Church must have a similar commitment, understanding that: *"The earnest, heartfelt, continuous prayer of a righteous man makes tremendous power available in its dynamic effects"* (Jas 5:16). Moreover, every committed Christian has this power, since our righteousness is in Christ Jesus: *"**Christ Jesus, who has become for us wisdom from God -- that is, our righteousness, holiness and redemption"*** (1 Cor 1:30).

Concerning the power of corporate prayer, God has promised: *"When I shut up the heavens so that there is no rain, or command locusts to devour the land or send a plague among my people,* **if my people, who are called by my name, will humble themselves and pray and seek my face and turn from their wicked ways, then will I hear from heaven and will forgive their sin and will heal their land.** *... My eyes will be open and my ears attentive to the prayers offered in this place"* 2 Chronicles 7:13-15

Regarding the power of our intercession for those who are not saved, He says: *"Submit to God and be at peace with him... pray to him, and he will hear you. ... He will deliver* **even the one who is not innocent, who will be delivered through the cleanness of your hands"** (Job 22: 21,27,30).

*"**A time is coming and has now come when the true worshipers will worship the Father in spirit and truth,** for they are the kind of worshipers the Father seeks. God is spirit, and his worshipers must worship in spirit and in truth"* (Jn 4:23-24).

God's children are indwelled by Holy Spirit, and: **"The Spirit helps us in our weakness. We do not know what we ought to pray for, but the Spirit himself intercedes for us with groans that words cannot express.** *And he who searches our hearts knows the mind of the Spirit, because the Spirit intercedes for the saints in accordance with God's will"* (Rom 8:26-27).

2) **The Word of God** -- the sword of the Spirit and the belt of
truth -- are among the weapons of spiritual warfare, and are particularly effective in evangelism and as a weapon of self defense against ignorance, deception, false doctrines, spiritual poverty, and walking outside God's will. David said, *"Wherewithal shall a young man cleanse his way? By taking heed thereto according to thy word. ...*

***I have hidden Your Word in my heart that I might not sin against you.** Praise be to you, O Lord; teach me your decrees"* (Ps 119:9 & 11). ... *"I will delight myself in thy statues: **I will not forget thy word.** Deal bountifully with thy servant, that I may live and keep thy word"* (Ps 119:16-17). *"So shall I have wherewith to answer him that reproacheth me: for I trust in thy word"* (vs 42).

3) **Fasting** -- a powerful weapon of spiritual warfare, effective against heavy oppression that prayer alone may not be sufficient to overcome) *"When [**not, if or in case**] you fast, put oil on your head and wash your face, so that it will not be obvious to men that you are fasting, but only to your Father, who is unseen; and your Father, who sees what is done in secret, will reward you openly"* (Mt 6:17-18).

On one occasion, Jesus' *"disciples asked him privately, "Why could we not cast it (the demon) out" And he said to them, "This kind cannot be driven out by anything but prayer **and** fasting"* (Mk 9:28-29; Mt 17: 21).

Concerning fasting, Isaiah declared: *"Is not this the kind of fasting I have chosen:* **to loose the chains of injustice and untie the cords of the yoke, to set the oppressed free and break every yoke?** *Is it not to share your food with the hungry and to provide the poor wanderer with shelter -- when you see the naked, to clothe him, and not to turn away from your own flesh and blood? Then your light will break forth like the dawn, and your healing will quickly appear; then your righteousness will go before you, and the glory of the Lord will be your rear guard. Then you will call, and the Lord will answer; you will cry for help, and he will say: Here am I"* (Is 58:6-9).

4) **Casting out unclean spirits** -- spirits living in people, not those in thin air (Mt 10:1, Mk 6:7,13, 16:17-18, Lk 9:1-2). Sound wisdom, and spiritual discernment is required when operating in this spiritual realm. **Notice carefully, in this area of ministry, we have direct confrontation with evil spirits, or demons.** This is the only area we have been given Christ's authorized "believers' authority" over evil spiritual forces. **Every other role in spiritual warfare involves our focus on God and doing our part, by walking in obedience.**

Concerning our authority in this area -- which is to be employed when directed by Holy Spirit -- we must understand that **"The reason the Son of God appeared was to destroy the devil's work"** (1 Jn 3:8). Christ subsequently appointed us to this task: *"As the Father has sent me,* **I am sending you**" (Jn 20:21). *"God anointed Jesus of Nazareth with the Holy Spirit and power, and how he went around doing good and healing all who were under the power of the devil, because God was with him"* (Acts 10:38). And, Jesus said: **"Anyone who has faith in me will do what I have been doing. He will do even greater things than these,** *because I am going to the Father"* (Jn 14:12).

Jesus said: *"From the time of Yochanan the Immerser [John the Baptist] until now, the Kingdom of Heaven has been suffering violence; yes, violent ones are trying to snatch it away"* (Mt 11:12 CJB). Yet, He has assured us: **"I have given you authority to trample on snakes and scorpions and to overcome all the power of the enemy;** *nothing will harm you"* (Lk 10:19). *"Do not be afraid or discouraged because of this vast army (of Satan). For the battle is not yours, but God's"* (2 Ch 20:15). *"The seventy-two,"* whom Christ sent out with instructions to heal the sick and deliver the oppressed, *"returned with joy and said, "Lord, even the demons submit to us in your name"* (Lk 10:17).

5) **Walking in obedience and consecration** -- which is the breastplate of righteousness -- is part of our spiritual armor and likewise one of our weapons of spiritual warfare against sin. *"Does the Lord delight in burnt offerings and sacrifices as much as in obeying the voice of the Lord?* **To obey is better than sacrifice,** *and to heed is better than the fat of rams"* (1 Sam 15:22)

Walking in obedience is the prerequisite for our being issued the other weapons of spiritual warfare. Jesus said: **"Seek first his kingdom and his righteousness, and all these things will be given to you as well"** (Mt 6:33-34). *"This is the one I esteem: he who is humble and contrite in spirit, and trembles at my word"* (Is 66:2).

King David, wrote: *"You do not delight in sacrifice, or I would bring it; you do not take pleasure in burnt offerings.* **The sacrifices of God are a broken spirit; a broken and contrite heart, O God, you will not despise"** (Ps 51:16-17).

And God promised us: *"When I shut up the heavens so that there is no rain, or command locusts to devour the land or send a plague among my people,* **if my people, who are called by my name, will humble themselves and pray and seek my face and turn from their wicked ways, then will I hear from heaven and will forgive their sin and will heal their land.** *Now my eyes will be open and my ears attentive to the prayers offered in this place"* (2 Ch 7:13-15).

Sometimes, we wonder why God does not act in our behalf. He says: **"If my people would but listen to me, if Israel would follow my ways, how quickly would I subdue** *their enemies and turn my hand against their foes"* (Ps 81:13-14). *"Submit to God and be at peace with him. ... pray to him, and he will hear you. ... He will deliver even the one who is not innocent, who will be delivered through the cleanness of your hands"* (Job 22: 21,27,30).

6) **Walking in love, repentance and forgiveness** -- the shoes of the gospel of peace -- are included both as part of our spiritual armor, and among our weapons of spiritual warfare, to be used against curses, sickness and hatred.

Regarding walking in love, we read: ***"By this all men will know that you are my disciples, if you love one another"*** (Jn 13:35). *"If I have a faith that can move mountains, but have not love, I am nothing. If I give all I possess to the poor and surrender my body to the flames, but have not love, I gain nothing"* (1 Co 13:2-3).

What kind, or measure, of love is demanded of us? *"This is how we know what love is: Jesus Christ laid down his life for us. And we ought to lay down our lives for our brothers"* (1 Jn 3:16). *"Let no debt remain outstanding, except the continuing debt to love one another, for he who loves his fellowman has fulfilled the law"* (Rom 13:8). *"Unless your righteousness surpasses that of the Pharisees and teachers of the law, you will certainly not enter the kingdom of heaven"* (Mt 5:20).

Walking in Repentance and Mercy -- repentance to God and mercy to one another.

We read first of mercy: ***"Because of the Lord's great love we are not consumed,*** *for his compassion never fails. They are new every morning; great is your faithfulness ..."* (Lam 3: 22-23). *"Let us then approach the throne of grace with confidence, so that we may receive mercy and find grace to help us in our time of need"* (Heb 4:16).

"Blessed are the merciful, for they will be shown mercy" (Mt 5:7). *"Forgive us our debts, as we also haveforgiven our debtors"* (Mt 6:12). *"Be merciful, just as your Father is merciful. Do not judge, and you will not be judged. Do not condemn, and you will not be condemned. Forgive, and you will be forgiven. Give, and it will be given to you. ... For with the measure you use, it will be measured to you"* (Lk 6:36-38).

Healing through Repentance: "Therefore confess your sins to each other and pray for each other so that you may be healed" (Jas 5:16). "Bless the Lord, O my soul, and forget not all his benefits, who forgives all your iniquity, who heals all your diseases" (Ps 103:1-3).

7) **Walking in fellowship** -- both with God and with man, is a key weapon in our spiritual warfare against spiritual unfruitfulness, spiritual weakness, spiritual poverty, sin, and deception. "Oh, for the days when I was in my prime, when God's intimate friendship blessed my house, when the Almighty was with me" (Job 29:4-5). Friendships with man, while essential, should not be entered into lightly. **"A righteous man is cautious in friendship"** (Pr 12:26). "Beloved, it is a fine and faithful work that you are doing when you give any service to the [Christian] brethren, and [especially when they are] strangers. They have testified before the church of your love and friendship" (3 Jn 5-6).

8) **Walking in agreement --** maintaining harmony with other brethren is among our most important weapons of spiritual warfare against division, conflict, unanswered prayers, etc.

In Word: "He who guards his mouth and his tongue keeps himself from calamity" (Pr 21:23). **"The tongue has the power of life and death**, and those who love it will eat its fruit" (Pr 18:21). "To man belong the plans of the heart, but from the Lord comes the reply of the tongue" (Pr 16:1). See also, (Mt 12:34-37).

In Deed: "Again, I tell you that if two of you on earth agree about anything you ask for, it will be done for you by my Father in heaven. For where two or three come together in my name, there am I with them" (Mt 18:19-20). "Two are better than one, because they have a good return for their work. If one falls down, his friend can help him up. But pity the man who falls and has no one to help him up!" (Eccl 4:9-10).

Agreement with another in the Lord makes a strong three strand cord: "Though one may be overpowered, two can defend themselves. **A cord of three strands is not quickly broken**" (Eccl 4:11). "Every matter must be established by the testimony of two or three witnesses" (Dt 19:15, Mt 18:16, 2 Cor 13:1).

9) ***Walking in humility*** -- humility is numbered among our important weapons of spiritual warfare, effective against pride, egoism, arrogance, disrespect. ***"The meek (humble) will inherit the land and enjoy great peace"*** (Ps 37:11). *"Blessed are the meek, for they will inherit the earth"* (Mt 5:5).

God has promised: ***"Ask of me, and I will make the nations your inheritance***, *the ends of the earth your possession"* (Ps 2:8). *"You will be called priests of the Lord. ...You will feed on the wealth of nations"* (Is 61:6). The Nations' wealth is our inheritance for our priestly duties. ***"A sinner's wealth is stored up for the righteous"*** (Pr 13:22). [There are two types of wealth envisioned here: the monetary wealth of the nations, and the value of her people -- which are priceless. The righteous are to use the monetary wealth, it to carry the gospel to the world, liberating the souls held captive.]

"Humility and the fear of the Lord bring wealth and honor and life" (Pr 22:4). ***"Humble yourselves before the Lord, and he shall exalt you"*** (Jas 4:10). *"God opposes the proud but gives grace to the humble"* (Jas 4:6, 1 Pet 5:5). *"A man's life is not his own; it is not for man to direct his steps"* (Jer 10:23). *"This is the one I esteem: he who is humble and contrite in spirit, and trembles at my word"* (Is 66:2). *"The sacrifices of God are a broken spirit; a broken and contrite heart, O God, you will not despise"* (Ps 51:17).

"Everything comes from you [O God], and we have given you only what comes from your hand" (1 Ch 29:14).

10) ***Walking in submission*** -- submission, or compliance, is a critical weapon in spiritual warfare, effective against self-ambition, self-glory, pride, disrespect, and competition. Submission to God is evident through compliance to God's Word and yielding to the guidance of indwelling Holy Spirit.

Submission -- "Submit yourselves, then, to God. Resist the devil, and he will flee from you" (Jas 4:7). *"Those who are led by the Spirit of God are sons of God"* (Rom 8:14). *"But if you are led by the Spirit, you are not under law. ... the fruit of the Spirit is love, joy, peace, patience, kindness, goodness, faithfulness, gentleness and self-control"* (Gal 5:18, 22-23). Jesus said: *"I am the vine; you are the branches. If a man remains in me and I in him, he will bear much fruit; without me you can do nothing"* (Jn 15:5).

Our effectiveness in spiritual warfare is enhanced when we operate *"Not by might nor by power, but by my Spirit"* (Zec 4:6). **Sobriety** -- *"**And do not be drunk with wine**, in which is dissipation; but **be filled with the Spirit**, speaking to one another in psalms and hymns and spiritual songs, singing and making melody in your heart to the Lord, giving thanks always for all things to God the Father in the name of our Lord Jesus Christ, submitting to one another in the fear of God"* (Eph 5:18-21).

*"**Endure hardship as discipline**; God is treating you as sons. For what son is not disciplined by his father? If you are not disciplined (and everyone undergoes discipline), then you are illegitimate children and not true sons. Moreover, we have all had human fathers who disciplined us and we respected them for it. How much more should we submit to the Father of our spirits and live!"* (Heb 12:7-9).

Submission, both to One Another and to those in Authority -- Especially to Spiritual Leaders; *"Submit to one another out of reverence for Christ"* (Eph 5:21). *"It is necessary to submit to the authorities, not only because of possible punishment but also because of conscience"* (Rom 13:5).

*"**Obey your leaders and submit to their authority**. They keep watch over you as men who must give an account. Obey them so that their work will be a joy, not a burden, for that would be of no advantage to you"* (Heb 13:17). *"Submit yourselves for the Lord's sake to every authority instituted among men"* (1 Pe 2:13).

11) **Holy communion** -- honoring the sacrifice of Jesus -- in body and blood -- by surrendering our body as a living sacrifice (Rom 12:1), and entering into His proffered exchange of blood for blood and soul for soul, is among our essential weapons of spiritual warfare, effective against all forms of evil.

"For my flesh is real food and my blood is real drink. Whoever eats my flesh and drinks my blood remains in me, and I in him" (John 6:55-56). *"The Lord Jesus, on the night he was betrayed, took bread, and when he had given thanks, he broke it and said, "This is my body, which is for you; do this in remembrance of me." In the same way, after supper he took the cup, saying, "This cup is the new covenant in my blood; do this, whenever me." you drink it, in remembrance*

of me. "For whenever you eat this bread and drink this cup, you proclaim the Lord's death until he comes" (1 Cor 11:23-26).

"In him we have redemption through his blood, the forgiveness of sins, in accordance with the riches of God's grace that he lavished on us with all wisdom and understanding" (Eph 1:7-8). *"They overcame him by the blood of the Lamb and by the word of their testimony; they did not love their lives so much as to shrink from death"* (Rev 12:11). *"Everyone born of God overcomes the world. This is the victory that has overcome the world, even our faith"* 1 Jn 5:4).

"The blood of goats and bulls and the ashes of a heifer sprinkled on those who are ceremonially unclean sanctify them so that they are outwardly clean. How much more, then, will the blood of Christ, who through the eternal Spirit offered himself unblemished to God, cleanse our consciences from acts that lead to death, so that we may serve the living God!" (Heb 9:13-14).

12) ***Anointing with oil*** –- anointing oil -- symbolic of the anointing of the Holy Spirit -- is among our weapons of spiritual warfare, effective against sickness, evil spirits, weakness and other spiritual burdens. The oil has no divine, mystical or magical power in and of itself. It is our faith and obedience, using it when and were necessary, that enables God to do miraculous works through us.

*"**When [not, if or in case]** you fast, put oil on your head and wash your face, so that it will not be obvious to men that you are fasting, but only to your Father, who is unseen; and your Father, who sees what is done in secret, will reward you openly"* (Mt 6:17-18).

Of Christ's disciples, it was noted: ***"They drove out many demons and anointed many sick people with oil and healed them"*** (Mk 6:13). [We are His disciples, and have been given the same anointing and power.] *"Is any one of you sick? He should call the elders of the church to pray over him and anoint him with oil in the name of the Lord"* (Jas 5:14).

Jesus said: *"The Spirit of the Lord is on me, because he has anointed me to preach good news to the poor. He has sent me to proclaim freedom for the prisoners and recovery of sight for the blind, to release the oppressed"* (Lk 4:18, Is 61:1).

"God anointed Jesus of Nazareth with the Holy Spirit and power, and he went around doing good and healing all who were under the power of the devil, because God was with him" (Acts 10:38).

The power of anointing -- *"And it shall come to pass in that day, that his burden shall be taken away from off thy shoulder, and his yoke from off thy neck, and the yoke shall be destroyed because of the anointing"* (Is 10:27). *"He (Moses) poured some of the anointing oil on Aaron's head and anointed him to consecrate him"* (Lev 8:12).

Directions for anointing -- *"Take the anointing oil and anoint him by pouring it on his head. Bring his sons and dress them in tunics and put headbands on them. Then tie sashes on Aaron and his sons. The priesthood is theirs by a lasting ordinance. In this way you shall ordain Aaron and his sons"* (Ex 29:7-9).

"And take some of the blood on the altar (now done by taking Holy communion) and some of the anointing oil and sprinkle it on Aaron and his garments and on his sons and their garments. Then he and his sons and their garments will be consecrated" (Ex 29:21).

Anoint church leaders and those ordained to service -- *"Anoint Aaron and his sons and consecrate them so they may serve me as priests. Say to the Israelites, "This is to be my sacred anointing oil for the generations to come. Do not pour it on men's bodies and do not make any oil with the same formula. It is sacred, and you are to consider it sacred. Whoever makes perfume like it and whoever puts it on anyone other than a priest must be cut off from his people"* (Ex 30:30-33).

"You anoint my head with oil; my cup overflows. Surely goodness and love will follow me all the days of my life, and I will dwell in the house of the Lord forever" (Ps 23:5-6). *"He allowed no one to oppress them; for their sake he rebuked kings: Do not touch my anointed ones; do my prophets no harm"* (Ps 105:14-15).

13) **Praise and thanksgiving** -- are among our essential weapons of spiritual warfare, and are effective against ingratitude, murmuring, complaining, a comparative attitude, doubt, fear, a "spirit of despair" or feeling of worthlessness (Is 61:4)). This includes listening to praise and worship music, offering prayers of thanksgiving for answered prayers, prayers of praise and worship, and maintaining a thankful, praise-filled, expressive lifestyle.

*"**May the praise of God be in their mouths and a double-edged sword in their hands,** to inflict vengeance on the nations and punishment on the peoples, to bind their kings with fetters, their nobles with shackles of iron, to carry out the sentence written against them. This is the glory of all his saints"* (Ps 149:6-9). ...

"Since my youth or God you have taught me and this day I will declare your marvelous deeds" (Ps 71:17). [As spiritual children we can reflect on the time since we got saved, remembering how God has kept us under his wing, since our spiritual youth. Our physical age has little or no relevance to our spiritual lives.]

*"**O come let us sing to the Lord; let us make a joyful noise to the rock of our salvation**: Let us come into his presence with thanksgiving"* (Ps 95:1-2). *"Rejoice in the Lord always; again I will say rejoice. Let all men know your forbearance (patience). The Lord is at hand. Have no anxiety about anything, but in everything by prayer and supplication with thanksgiving let your request be made known to God. And the peace of God, which passes all understanding, will keep your hearts and your minds in Christ Jesus"* (Phil 4:4-7).

"I urge that supplications, prayers, intercessions, and thanksgiving be made for all men" (1 Ti 2:1). *"Do not be grieved for, the joy of the Lord is your strength"* (Neh 8:10).

14) ***Positive confession and guarding the tongue*** -- this is among our most important weapons of spiritual warfare, effective against pessimism, self-proclaimed calamities -- spiritual, social, physical, material, etc. -- and for calling into reality our desires that are in agreement with God's plans and purposes"

> 1. Removing mountains (obstacles in life which may be physical, circumstances, emotional, spiritual, social, financial (Luke 6: 45 Mt 17:20, 21:21).
> 2. Dealing with calamity (Pro 21: 23, 13: 3).
> 3. Binding the powers of darkness, and loosing the blessings of God (Mt 16:19).
> 4. The power of the tongue to speak life and death -- spiritual, physical, social, material and financial (Pro 18:20-21).
> 5. The power of the tongue to release or withhold God's blessings, effecting destiny (Jas 3: 3-6; Pro 13:2; 18:7).

14) **Positive confession and guarding the tongue** -- this is among our most important weapons of spiritual warfare, effective against pessimism, self-proclaimed calamities -- spiritual, social, physical, material, etc. -- and for calling into reality our desires that are in agreement with God's plans and purposes.

1. Removing mountains (obstacles in life which may be physical, circumstances, emotional, spiritual, social, financial (Luke 6: 45 Mt 17:20, 21:21).
2. Dealing with calamity (Pro 21: 23, 13: 3).
3. Binding the powers of darkness, and loosing the blessings of God (Mt 16:19).
4. The power of the tongue to speak life and death -- spiritual, physical, social, material and financial (Pro 18:20-21).
5. The power of the tongue to release or withhold God's blessings, effecting destiny (Jas 3: 3-6; Pro 13:2; 18:7).

15) **Faithfulness in tithing and generosity in giving to the work within the body of Christ** – this is among our essential weapons of spiritual warfare, effective against greed, selfishness, insufficiency and poverty.

"Honor the Lord with your wealth, with the first fruits of all your crops; then your barns will be filled to overflowing, and your vats will brim over with new wine" (Pro 3:9-10). ... *"Bring the whole tithe into the storehouse ... and see if I will not throw open the floodgates of heaven and pour out so much blessing that you will not have room enough for it. I will prevent pests from devouring your crops ... says the Lord Almighty"* (Mal 3:10-11).

"Command them to do good, to be rich in good deeds, and to be generous and willing to share. In this way they will lay up (in heaven) treasure for themselves as a firm foundation for the coming age, so that they may take hold of the life that is truly life" (1 Ti 6:18-19). *"The blessing of the Lord brings wealth, and he adds no trouble to it"* (Pro 10:22).

16) **The name of Jesus and our position in Christ** -- the helmet of salvation serves both as a part of our spiritual armor and as a weapon of spiritual warfare, protecting us against every curse and work of the enemy.
   • **The name of Jesus** -- *"Therefore God exalted him to the highest place and gave him the name that is above every name, that **at the name of Jesus every knee should***

bow, in heaven and on earth and under the earth, *and every tongue confess that Jesus Christ is Lord, to the glory of God the Father"* (Phil 2:9-11).

- *The seventy-two returned with joy and said,* "**Lord, even the demons submit to us in your name**" *(Lk 10:17). "Worthy is the Lamb, who was slain, to receive power and wealth and wisdom and strength and honor and glory and praise!"* (Rev 5:12).

- **Our position in Christ** -- **"Therefore, if anyone is in Christ, he is a new creation; the old has gone, the new has come!** *All this is from God, who reconciled us to himself through Christ and gave us the ministry of reconciliation"* (2 Cor 5:17-18).

- *"Therefore,* **there is now no condemnation for those who are in Christ Jesus**, *because through Christ Jesus the law of the Spirit of life set me free from the law of sin and death"* (Rom 8:1-2).

- *"***Christ redeemed us from the curse of the law by becoming a curse for us**, *for it is written: "Cursed is everyone who is hung on a tree." He redeemed us in order that the blessing given to Abraham might come to the Gentiles through Christ Jesus, so that by faith we might receive the promise of the Spirit"* (Gal 3:13-14).

- *"God made him who had no sin to be sin for us, so that in him we might become the righteousness of God"* (2 Cor 5:21).

- *"***You are all sons of God through faith in Christ Jesus**... *There is neither Jew nor Greek, slave nor free, male nor female, for you are all one in Christ Jesus. If you belong to Christ, then you are Abraham's seed, and heirs according to the promise"* (Gal 3:26,28-29).

- *"This mystery is that through the gospel the Gentiles are heirs together with Israel, members together of one body, and sharers together in the promise in Christ Jesus"* (Eph 3:6).

- *"Praise be to the God and Father of our Lord Jesus Christ, who has blessed us in the heavenly realms with every spiritual blessing in Christ. ...*

- *In him we have redemption through his blood, the forgiveness of sins, in accordance with the riches of God's grace that he lavished on us with all wisdom and understanding"* (Eph 1:3,7-8).

73

17) **Faith-the spiritual shield** -- the shield of faith is among the articles of our spiritual armor and warfare, and is effective against doubt, fear, the "spirit of despair" (Is 61:4), giving up, walking by sight and displeasing God. *"Even youths grow tired and weary, and young men stumble and fall; but those who hope in the Lord will renew their strength. They will soar on wings like eagles; they will run and not grow weary, they will walk and not be faint"* (Is 40-30-31).

18) **Hard work** -- is an essential weapon of spiritual warfare, combating spiritual laziness, stagnation, neglecting the utilization of our God given talents. It is also an effective weapon against the lack of promotion in God's kingdom. *"The man with the two talents also came. Master,' he said, you entrusted me with two talents; see, I have gained two more.' His master replied, Well done, good and faithful servant! You have been faithful with a few things; I will put you in charge of many things. Come and share your master's happiness!"* (Mt 25:22-23).

19) **Persistence or Perseverance** -- an essential weapon of spiritual warfare, combating impatience, despair, lack of commitment, and lack of obligation. *"**God will give to each person according to what he has done." To those who by persistence in doing good seek glory, honor and immortality, he will give eternal life.** But for those who are self-seeking and who reject the truth and follow evil, there will be wrath and anger"* (Rom 2:6-8).

- *"Let us not become weary in doing good, for at the proper time we will reap a harvest if we do not give up"* (Gal 6:9; Lk 11:5-8).

20) **Planning** -- an essential weapon of spiritual warfare, effective against having no clear direction in life, a sense of purposelessness, meaninglessness, worthlessness, failure of plans God plants in our hearts that languish for lack of action, personal failure, wasted resources (time, talents, strength, finances, etc.), and living a trial and error lifestyle.

- *"**Commit your plans to God and they will succeed**"* (Pro 16:6). *"Commit to the Lord whatever you do, and your plans will succeed"* (Pro 16:3).

- *"Many are the plans in the mind of a man, but it is the purpose of the Lord that will be established"* (Pro 19:21).

21) **Prayer Partners** -- having one or more prayer partners is one of the essential protective pieces of weaponry in our spiritual armor. *"I tell you that if two of you on earth agree about anything you ask for, it will be done for you by my Father in heaven. For where two or three come together in my name, there am I with them"* (Mt 18:19-20).

22) **Ministry Partners** -- having a ministry partner is another protective weapon. Jesus, *"Calling the Twelve to him, he sent them out two by two and gave them authority over evil spirits"* (Mk 6:7).

23) **God's Promises** -- God's promises are an essential defensive weapon against all the wiles of the powers of darkness, in that they both equip us, and enable us to participate in Christ's divine nature. *"God's power has given us everything we need for life and godliness, through our knowing the One who called us to his own glory and goodness. By these **he has given us valuable and superlatively great promises, so that through them you might come to share in God's nature** and escape the corruption which evil desires have brought into the world. ... Thus you will be generously supplied with everything you need to enter the eternal Kingdom of our Lord and Deliverer, Yeshua the Messiah"* (2 Pe 1:3-4 & 11).

The number and scope of God's promises is so great, we have devoted an entire chapter to this spiritual weapon. And, since the number of biblical promises is such that even devoting an entire chapter to them, we barely touch them, we encourage you to avail yourselves of one or more books on the promises of the Bible.

Personal Application: ~ Score your believed proficiency in the use of each of the spiritual weapons?

Ex.	Good	Fair	Poor	Spiritual Weapon
[ ]	[ ]	[ ]	[ ]	Prayer
[ ]	[ ]	[ ]	[ ]	The Word of God
[ ]	[ ]	[ ]	[ ]	Fasting
[ ]	[ ]	[ ]	[ ]	Casting out unclean spirits
[ ]	[ ]	[ ]	[ ]	Walking in obedience & consecration
[ ]	[ ]	[ ]	[ ]	Walk in love, repentance & forgiveness
[ ]	[ ]	[ ]	[ ]	Walking in fellowship
[ ]	[ ]	[ ]	[ ]	Walking in agreement
[ ]	[ ]	[ ]	[ ]	Walking in humility

[ ]	[ ]	[ ]	[ ]	
[ ]	[ ]	[ ]	[ ]	Walking in submission
[ ]	[ ]	[ ]	[ ]	Participation in holy communion
[ ]	[ ]	[ ]	[ ]	Anointing with oil
[ ]	[ ]	[ ]	[ ]	Praise and thanksgiving
[ ]	[ ]	[ ]	[ ]	Positive confession/guarding tongue
[ ]	[ ]	[ ]	[ ]	Faithfulness in tithing & offerings
[ ]	[ ]	[ ]	[ ]	The Name of, & your position of Christ
[ ]	[ ]	[ ]	[ ]	The spiritual shield of faith
[ ]	[ ]	[ ]	[ ]	Hard work of ministry
[ ]	[ ]	[ ]	[ ]	Persistence or perseverance
[ ]	[ ]	[ ]	[ ]	Planning ministry activities
[ ]	[ ]	[ ]	[ ]	Relying on & claiming God's promises
[ ]	[ ]	[ ]	[ ]	Prayer partner
[ ]	[ ]	[ ]	[ ]	Ministry partner

Repentance:

"Do all you can to present yourself to God as someone worthy of his approval, as a worker with no need to be ashamed, because he deals straightforwardly with the Word of the Truth" (2 Ti 2:15-16 CJB).

"Therefore this is what the Lord says: "If you repent, I will restore you that you may serve me; if you utter worthy, not worthless, words, you will be my spokesman" (Jer 15:19).

"Those whom I love I rebuke and discipline. So be earnest, and repent" (Rev 3:19).

Ministry:

Confess failures in spiritual warfare -- *"If we confess our sins, he is faithful and just and will forgive us our sins and purify us from all unrighteousness. If we claim we have not sinned, we make him out to be a liar and his word has no place in our lives"* (1 John 1:9-10). ~ **Seek God's Healing** -- *"Return, backsliding children, and I will heal your backsliding." "Here we are, we are coming to you, for you are Adonai our God"* (Jer 3:22).

Accept Christ's Commission -- *"He has committed to us the message of reconciliation. We are therefore Christ's ambassadors, as though God were making His appeal through us"* (2 Cor 5:19).

Accept His appointment -- *"See, today I appoint you over nations and kingdoms to uproot and tear down, to destroy and overthrow, to build and to plant"* (Jer 1:9-10).

Accept His Anointing -- *"Anoint them just as you anointed their father, so they may serve me as priests"* (Ex 40:15).

Chapter Five ~ Praying in Power

The Symphony of Spiritual Warfare:
"If two of you on earth agree (harmonize together, or make a symphony together about whatever [anything and everything] *they ask, it will come to pass for them by my Father in heaven.*

Making Music Unto the Lord:
For wherever two or three are gathered (drawn together as My followers) in (into) My name, there I AM in the midst of them" (Mt 18:19-20). The Greek word used in the first sentence of this text, that has been translated into English as *agree*, is actually a musical term.

The concept it conveys is one of harmony, rapport, balance and unity. In the second sentence, the term *gathered together* literally means they 'have been led together'.

Spiritual Guidance:
The phrase speaking of being led together, poses the question: led by whom? God's word answers this, saying: *"If you live according to [the dictates of] the flesh, you will surely die. But, if through the power of the [Holy] Spirit, you are [habitually] putting to death (making extinct, deadening) the [evil] deeds prompted by the body, you shall [really and genuinely] live forever. For all who are led by the Spirit of God are sons of God.*

"For [the Spirit which] you have now received [is] not a spirit of slavery to put you once more in bondage to fear, but you have received the Spirit of adoption [the Spirit producing sonship] in [the bliss of] which we cry, Abba (Father)! Father! The Spirit Himself [thus] testifies together with our own spirit, [assuring us] that we are children of God. And if we are [His] children, then we are [His] heirs also: heirs of God and fellow heirs with Christ [sharing His inheritance with Him]; only we must share His suffering if we are to share His glory" (Rom 8:13-17).

In the natural, when prayer partners are led together by Holy Spirit, thus brought into unity, one beholds a beautiful symphony of souls in agreement. Considering what we learned in chapter one, about the music and color emitted by one's DNA, imagine what God must see -- the souls of His children presenting a panoply of brilliant colors and harmonizing music! As God's children -- members of His family [His Body: the church], led by Holy Spirit, **"we have been made a spectacle (a beautiful display) to the whole universe, to angels as well as men"** (1 Co 4:9).

The early church apparently understood this. *"They all joined together constantly in prayer"* (Acts 1:14); and, *"they raised their voices together in prayer to God. "Sovereign Lord," they said, "you made the heaven and the earth and the sea, and everything in them"* (Acts 4:24). Paul, an apostle, understood this principle, and said: *"I want men everywhere to lift up holy hands in prayer"* (1 Tim 2:8).

No other situation or circumstance in life demands more unity -- more harmony and perseverance -- than spiritual warfare. In spiritual warfare, we are fighting against unseen principalities and powers. *"We wrestle not against flesh and blood but against principalities, powers, against the rulers of the darkness of this world, against spiritual wickedness in high places"* (Eph 6:12).

Symphonic Instruments:
Just as a symphony is comprised of numerous musical instruments All playing in harmony, so it is with effective prayer. There are Numerous kinds of prayer, which when harmonized, give an Individual or church, far more power than relying on a single Instrument, or single type of prayer. Learning to play each Instrument well – becoming competent in each type of prayer – Which equips one to *"pray in the spirit on all occasions with all Kinds of prayers and requests"* (Eph 6:18).

Many Christians don't even realize that there are different kinds of prayer. But, according to this verse, God has ordained many types of prayer – specialities, as it were – that are available to us, to use as needed. These various types of prayer include, but are not limited to the following:

• ***The Prayer of Agreement*** -- The instrument of agreement is essential. After telling the church that Christ appointed some as apostles, others as prophets, and still others as evangelists, pastors and teachers, he explained their purpose -- *"to prepare God's people for works of service, **so that the body of Christ may be built up,** until we all reach unity in the faith **and in the knowledge of the Son of God,** and become mature (Christians), attaining to the whole measure of the fullness of Christ"* (Eph 4:10-13).

*"I tell you that if two of you here on earth **agree** about anything people ask, it will be for them from my Father in heaven. For wherever two or three are assembled in my name, I am there with them"* (Mt 18:19-20). The importance of agreement is further highlighted by the apostle, Paul.

*"I appeal to you, brothers, in the name of our Lord Jesus Christ, that all of you **agree** with one another so that there may be no divisions among you and that you may **be perfectly united in mind and thought"*** (1 Cor 1:10-11).

*"I plead with E____ and I plead with S____ to **agree** with each other in the Lord"* (Phil 4:2).

- **The Prayer of Blessing** -- This is a small but powerful instrument in the symphony of prayer -- an instrument that is used far too infrequently, particularly in our own families and circle of friends. The Lord, through Moses, gave Israel specific instructions concerning the use of this instrument.

"The Lord said to Moses, "Tell Aaron and his sons, 'This is how you are to bless the Israelites. Say to them: "The Lord bless you and keep you; the Lord make his face shine upon you and be gracious to you; the Lord turn his face toward you and give you peace." So they will put my name on the Israelites, and I will bless them" (Num 6:22-27).

- God enumerated six blessings that we can pray over our children and over others whom we wish to bless:
    1) The Lord bless you,

    2) (The Lord) keep you,

    3) (The Lord) makes His face shine upon you

    4) (The Lord) be gracious to you.

    5) (The Lord) lift up His countenance upon you,

    6) (The Lord) give you peace.

If we are faithful in using this instrument -- the prayer of blessing -- God has promised to increase our blessings by adding His own. *"So they will put my name on the Israelites, and I will bless them"* (vs 27).

While our blessings are important to our children, our resources are finite, but God's are unlimited. Parents, pray blessings over your children and see what the Lord will do!

- **The Prayer of Cursing** -- This may seem like an odd instrument to include in the symphony of prayer, however, Christians are charged not only with the responsibility to bless, but with the responsibility to curse when appropriate. Curses are the flip-side of blessings. In other words, the withholding of blessings is a curse; and there are certainly many individuals on whom it would be inappropriate to pronounce blessings. This being said, this instrument is to be used sparingly, since it does not give us a license to call down devastation on whomever one pleases, whenever one pleases.

Jesus provided clear instructions for the use of this instrument when he cursed the fig tree that was covered with leaves but had no fruit (Mt 21). *"Seeing a fig tree by the road, he went up to it but found nothing on it except leaves. Then he said to it, "May you never bear fruit again!" Immediately the tree withered"* (Mt 21:19). The fig tree was not producing fruit, its designed purpose. It was in a sense deceptive since fig trees are deciduous and put on their fruit before they leaf out. Thus, it would have been inappropriate to bless the tree -- since it yielded no fruit, deceiving him, and no doubt others.

Similarly, when we encounter an individual who is not walking in the Lord, or not living up to the light that they have been given, it would be inappropriate to bless them. They are living a lie, and for us to bless them would be to enable their deception. In such cases, it is most appropriate to withhold our blessings, which by definition, is declaring a curse upon them. This is the covert, or secret use of this instrument. However, there is also the more overt, or straightforward use, such as Jesus cursing the fig tree.

To illustrate how one might appropriately employ this instrument in this manner, let us share a personal experience. While living in Hawaii, we were, in addition to counseling, serving as the associate pastors of a local church. Over time, the counseling load in our clinic increased to the point that we had to make a choice, and we knew that the Lord had called us -- first and foremost -- to counsel. We prayerfully sought the Lord, and felt directed not only to step aside from the role as associate pastor, but to leave the church we had been pastoring, so that no one would be confused as to who the pastor was.

After receiving the answer, we invited our associate pastor and the deacons out to our home one evening to share our decision. We shared a time of tears and joy, knowing it was the right decision, but grieving the loss of the relationship we had shared.

Subsequent to stepping aside as associate pastor of that church, we were asked to fill the role of itinerant pastors among the Pentecostal church fellowship, assisting those pastors who were on vacation or ill. It was a role that was not too demanding and enjoyable, giving an added opportunity – to strengthen our relationships with the other pastors, which was important in our role as pastoral counselors serving the body of Christ at large.

In this capacity, while ministering at one local church, the members shared their dilemma at being located immediately across the street from a bar that was not only extremely noisy; it was also a place where drugs were sold and exchanged. Even worse, its patrons often left the bar, stumbled across the street and urinated or defecated on the church property. The pastor and elders had on numerous occasions spoken to the bar owner, whose response was: "If you don't like it, then move!"

Not believing that this was an acceptable solution, we prayed with the church and God gave clear instructions that we were to curse the bar, as Jesus did the fig tree (Mt 11:14). For prayer power, we invited the entire Pentecostal pastoral fellowship to assemble there for their midweek luncheon meetings. Convening together, we began praying against a bar that had been there for more than forty years, and was -- financially speaking -- the most stable salon establishment in the city. In the middle of the night, following our fifth midweek prayer service, the bar -- a brick and mortar building -- burned to the ground! The Lord had heard our prayers and answered in His own way!

- **_The Prayer of Command --_** The instrument of command leads one into a different arena -- one in which it both necessary and appropriate to take command, speaking with power and authority in Christ.

To illustrate situations when it is appropriate to rely on this instrument, consider the following: Joshua was engaged in a critical battle against the Amorites -- enemies of Israel. The Israelites were winning but night was falling and Joshua feared that if the battle was not concluded, they would return to fight another day. Joshua, confident that God had directed them to engage the Amorites, spoke to the Lord, saying:

"O sun, stand still over Gibeon, O moon, over the Valley of Aijalon."
So the sun stood still, and the moon stopped, till the nation
avenged itself on its enemies, as it is written in the Book of Jashar.
The sun stopped in the middle of the sky and delayed going down
about a full day. There has never been a day like it before nor since,
a day when the Lord listened to a man. Surely the Lord was fighting
for Israel!" (Josh 10:12-14).

Jesus also employed this instrument of prayer when he commanded
the barren fig tree to wither and die. *"Early in the morning, Jesus*
was on his way back to Jerusalem. He was hungry. He saw a fig
tree by the road. He went up to it but found nothing on it except
leaves. Then he said to it, "May you never bear fruit again!" Right
away the tree dried up. When the disciples saw this, they were
amazed. "How did the fig tree dry up so quickly?" they asked. Jesus
replied, "What I'm about to tell you is true. You must have faith
and not doubt. Then you can do what was done to the fig tree. And
you can say to this mountain, 'Go and throw yourself into the sea.'
It will be done. If you believe, you will receive what you ask for
when you pray" (Mt 21:18-22 NIrV).

James, in his epistle, affirms that the prayer of command is an
appropriate instrument to play. He recalls Elijah's victory over 450
prophets of Baal on Mount Carmel when, Elijah and the prophets
of Baal gathered with the people to settle the matter of deity --
whether Yahweh or Baal. The prophets of Baal beseeched him from
sunrise to dusk, without avail. Elijah began taunting them,
suggesting the Baal might be hard of hearing.

Then, after saturating Yahweh's sacrifice and the altar with water;
"at the time of [evening] sacrifice, the prophet Elijah stepped
forward and prayed: *"O Lord, God of Abraham, Isaac and Israel,*
let it be known today that you are God in Israel and that I am your
servant and have done all these things at your command. Answer
me, OLord, answer me, so these people will know that you, O Lord,
are God, and that you are turning their hearts back again" (1 Kings
18:36-37).

Concerning this, James, speaking to the early church, wrote: *"The*
prayer of a righteous person is powerful and effective. Eliyahu was
only a human being like us; yet he prayed fervently that it might
not rain, and no rain fell on the Land for three years and six months.
Then he prayed again, and heaven gave rain, and the Land
produced its crops" (Jas 5:16-18 CJB). Notice that these prayers
were all directed at proving God's divinity to doubters and scoffers.
Fervent prayer, when directed toward establishing Jehovah as God
Almighty, still produces the same results.

- **The Prayer of Commitment --** It is very important that every Christian become confident in the use of the instrument of commitment. Unlike other instruments, its use is like a single blast from a tuba or baritone, rather than the repetitive notes from a trumpet or cornet. That is, its effectiveness lies in its sincerity rather than in its repetition -- when we commit a situation into the Lord's hands we are to take our hands off the outcome.

  For example, David prayed: *"Into your hands I commit my spirit; redeem me, O Lord, the God of truth"* (Ps 31:5). Understanding the effectiveness of this, David counseled his readers to: *"Delight yourself in the Lord and he will give you the desires of your heart. **Commit** your way to the Lord; trust in him and he will do this: He will make your righteousness shine like the dawn, the justice of your cause like the noonday sun"* (Ps 37:4-6).

  David's son, King Solomon counseled: *"Commit to the LORD whatever you do, and your plans will succeed"* (Pro 16:3).

  Paul discovered the effectiveness of employing prayers of commitment rather than prayers of perseverance, when appropriate, saying: *"Remember that for three years I never stopped warning each of you night and day with tears. Now I commit you to God and to the word of his grace, which can build you up and give you an inheritance among all those who are sanctified"* (Acts 20:31-33).

  The apostle, Peter, understood the use of this instrument. To those suffering persecution, he wrote: *"So then, those who suffer according to God's will should commit themselves to their faithful Creator and continue to do good"* (1 Peter 4:19).

- **The Prayer of Consecration --** The instrument of consecration of devotion, is an instrument reserved for spiritual warriors who have made the commitment of surrendering their body a living sacrifice (Rom 12:2). This role in the symphony of ministry dates back to the Old Testament.

  God instructed Israel: *"I am the Lord your God; consecrate yourselves and be holy, because I am holy"* (Lev 11:44). ... *"Consecrate yourselves and be holy, because I am the Lord your God. Keep my decrees and follow them. I am the Lord, who makes you holy"* (Lev 20:7-8).

The act of consecrating, or devoting one's self to God is a prerequisite for God using a person to demonstrate His signs and wonders. Joshua advised the Israelites: *"Consecrate yourselves, for tomorrow the Lord will do amazing things among you"* (Josh 3:5).

Those involved in this ministry of spiritual warfare, as well as the temple, tabernacle, or church in which they serve, are to be consecrated – devoted – to God's solitary, unique service. *"Now devote your heart and soul to seeking the Lord your God"* (1 Ch 22:19). ... *"Consecrate yourselves now and consecrate the temple of the Lord, the God of your fathers. Remove all defilement from the sanctuary"* (2 Ch 29:5).

Job spoke of the blessings that one attains through consecrating themselves to God, saying: *"If you devote your heart to him and stretch out your hands to him, if you put away the sin that is in your hand and allow no evil to dwell in your tent, then you will lift up your face without shame; you will stand firm and without fear. You will surely forget your trouble, recalling it only as waters gone by"* (Job 11:13-16).

Jesus, demonstrating that it was still a viable thing to do, said: *"My Father, if it is possible, may this cup be taken from me. Yet not as I will, but as you will"* (Mt 26:39). ... The apostle, Paul, verified that such a commitment is still possible and desirable in our New Testament era – particularly in the ministry of prayer. *"Devote yourselves to prayer, being watchful and thankful"* (Col 4:2-3).

The Prayer of Declaration -- This instrument is vital in reaching the lost -- it involves a prayerful declaration of God's marvelous deeds, His mercy, kindness and love, to a hurting generation. Key Scriptures that reference the employment of this instrument include the following:

"Declare his glory among the nations, his marvelous deeds among all peoples" (1 Ch 16:24). ... *"O Lord, open my lips, and my mouth will declare your praise"* (Ps 51:15). ... *"Since my youth, O God, you have taught me, and to this day I declare your marvelous deeds"* (Ps 71:17.) ... *"I will declare that your love stands firm forever, that you established your faithfulness in heaven itself"* (Ps 89:2). ... *"I will declare your name to my brothers; in the presence of the congregation I will sing your praises"* (Heb 2:12).

- **The Prayer of Dedication --** This instrument is similar to commitment since both make the Lord the object of our prayer. The difference between them is that the prayer of commitment is a prayer offering ourselves, our talents and giftings, to the Lord. In contrast, the prayer of dedication, is used to devote ourselves, or something we have been given stewardship over, to the Lord. An example, is when one chooses to consecrate, or dedicate one's self to a particular ministry or calling that God has put on your heart.

Dedicating one's self, or something under one's stewardship to the Lord, is comparable to the concept of sanctification: that is, in purifying and setting one's self, or something, apart for holy purposes. For example, Samson was set apart to God at birth, his live dedicated to delivering Israel from the Philistines.

"The angel of the Lord appeared to her [his mother] and said, "You are sterile and childless, but you are going to conceive and have a son. Now see to it that you drink no wine or other fermented drink and that you do not eat anything unclean, because you will conceive and give birth to a son. No razor may be used on his head, because the boy is to be a Nazirite, **set apart to God from birth***, and he will begin the deliverance of Israel from the hands of the Philistines"* (Jdg 13:3-5).

Aaron and his descendants were **set apart**, or dedicated, to the Levitical Priesthood. *"Aaron was set apart, he and his descendants forever, to consecrate the most holy things, to offer sacrifices before the Lord, to minister before him and to pronounce blessings in his name forever"* (1 Ch 23:13).

The sons of Asaph were set apart, or dedicated to the ministry of prophetic music. *"David, together with the commanders of the army,* **set apart** *some of the sons of Asaph, Heman and Jeduthun for the ministry of prophesying, accompanied by harps, lyres and cymbals"* (1 Ch 25:1).

The fact that this setting-apart, or dedication, involved prayer, is evident in the dedication of Barnabas and Saul. *"In the church at Antioch there were prophets and teachers: Barnabas, Simeon called Niger, Lucius of Cyrene, Manaen (who had been brought up with Herod the tetrarch) and Saul. While they were worshiping the Lord and fasting, the Holy Spirit said,* **"Set apart for me Barnabas and Saul** *for the work to which I have called them." So* **after they had fasted and prayed, they placed their hands on them** *and sent them off"* (Acts 13:1-3).

The sons of Asaph were set apart, or dedicated to the ministry of prophetic music. *"David, together with the commanders of the army, **set apart** some of the sons of Asaph, Heman and Jeduthun for the ministry of prophesying, accompanied by harps, lyres and cymbals"* (1 Ch 25:1).

The fact that this setting-apart, or dedication, involved prayer, is evident in the dedication of Barnabas and Saul. *"In the church at Antioch there were prophets and teachers: Barnabas, Simeon called Niger, Lucius of Cyrene, Manaen (who had been brought up with Herod the tetrarch) and Saul. While they were worshiping the Lord and fasting, the Holy Spirit said, "**Set apart for me Barnabas and Saul** for the work to which I have called them." So **after they had fasted and prayed, they placed their hands on them** and sent them off"* (Acts 13:1-3).

The most important incident of the sanctification, dedication and setting apart of an individual involved Christ. Jesus, answering an accusation the Jews lodged against him, responded by quoting from the Old Testament: *"Scripture cannot be broken — what about the one whom the Father set apart as his very own and sent into the world?"* (John 10:35-36).

Concerning Jesus dedication, the author of Hebrews wrote: *"The Lord has sworn and will not change his mind: 'You are a priest forever.'" Because of this oath, Jesus has become the guarantee of a better covenant. Now there have been many of those priests, since death prevented them from continuing in office; but because Jesus lives forever, he has a permanent priesthood. Therefore he is able to save completely those who come to God through him, because he always lives to intercede for them. Such a high priest meets our need — one who is holy, blameless, pure, **set apart** from sinners, exalted above the heavens"* (Heb 7:21-26).

Sanctification and dedication are inseparable: God must initiate the call upon one's life; and that person must voluntarily respond, dedicating themselves to that calling, being thereafter set apart by the elders of the church through prayer and the laying on of hands (Acts 13:3).

- **The Prayer of Faith or Reception** -- This symphonic instrument is one of the most misunderstood, and therefore the most misused, or under-used, instrument of all. Its proper use is illustrated in the story of the widow whose son Elisha had -- through prayer -- revived from death. Some time later, her husband died and she was in danger of losing their house.

Remembering Elisha, the man of God, she entreated him to come to her aid.

"Elisha replied to her, "How can I help you? Tell me, what do you have in your house?" "Your servant has nothing there at all," she said, "except a little oil." Elisha said, "Go around and ask all your neighbors for empty jars. Don't ask for just a few. Then go inside and shut the door behind you and your sons. Pour oil into all the jars, and as each is filled, put it to one side." She left him and afterward shut the door behind her and her sons. They brought the jars to her and she kept pouring. When all the jars were full, she said to her son, "Bring me another one." But he replied, "There is not a jar left." Then the oil stopped flowing" (2 Kings 4:2-6).

This is not just an Old Testament story, or provision limited to the old covenant. Jesus repeatedly assured his disciples that His father in heaven would meet their needs. In assuring them, he also highlighted certain conditions. He said: *"**If you believe**, you will receive **whatever you ask for** in prayer"* (Mt 21:22). ... *"I tell you, **whatever you ask for in prayer, believe that you have received it, and it will be yours**"* (Mk 11:24-25).

The A, B. C's of Answered Prayer:
In these Scriptures, Jesus presents the A,B,C's of using this instrument -- the prayer of faith:

A = ask (according to His declared will)

B = believe His Word (deeming it a fact that you have received it -- past tense)

C = claim what God has promised – making a requisition for whatever you asked. This is similar to having funds deposited in your account. If you don't believe it is there and never write a check on that account, the funds will do you no good).

Unfortunately, many Christians, although they have read, or heard the story of the widow whose financial problems were solved by a miracle; and being familiar with the promises of God, think that they have a right to demand whatever God has promised, and they claim. However, Scripture has a good deal to say about how to use this instrument -- the prayer of faith – correctly.

Jesus said: *"And **when you pray, do not keep on babbling** like pagans, for they think they will be heard because of their many* *"words. Do not be like them, for **your Father knows what you need before you ask him.** This, then, is how you should pray:Our Father in heaven, hallowed be your name, your kingdom come, your will be done on earth as it is in heaven. **Give us today our daily bread.** Forgive us our debts, as we also have forgiven our debtors. And lead us not into temptation, but deliver us from the evil one"* (Mt 6:7-13).

Other directions for using this instrument are provided by the apostles. James wrote: *"But when he asks, he must **believe and not doubt**, because he who doubts is like a wave of the sea, blown and tossed by the wind. That man should not think he will receive anything from the Lord; 8 he is a double-minded man, unstable in all he does"* (Jas 1:7-8). ... *"When you ask, **you do not receive, because you ask with wrong motives, that you may spend what you get on your pleasures (lust)**"* (Jas 4:3).

The apostle, John, points out two additional prerequisites for successfully using this instrument: to have a clean heart; and to walk in obedience. *"Dear friends, if our hearts do not condemn us, we have confidence before God and receive from him anything we ask, because we obey his commands and do what pleases him"* (1 Jn 3:21-23). Two other prerequisites are: having confidence in God and our position in Him; and limiting our petitions to those things that are according to His will. *"This is the confidence we have in approaching God: that if we ask anything according to his will, he hears us. And if we know that he hears us — whatever we ask — we know that we have what we asked of him"* (1 Jn 5:14-15).

If we fulfill these prerequisites, the blessings and benefits of the prayer of faith are almost unlimited. The apostle, Luke, emphasizes this, writing: *"So I say to you: Ask and it will be given to you; seek and you will find; knock and the door will be opened to you. For everyone who asks receives; he who seeks finds; and to him who knocks, the door will be opened. "Which of you fathers, if your son asks for a fish, will give him a snake instead? Or if he asks for an egg, will give him a scorpion? If you then, though you are evil, know how to give good gifts to your children, how much more will your Father in heaven give the Holy Spirit to those who ask him!"* (Lk 11:9-13). The all inclusiveness of the prayer of faith is inferred throughout the Scriptures, in texts such as those following:

- *"If any of you lacks wisdom, he should ask God, who gives generously to all without finding fault, and it will be given to him"* (Jas 1:5-8).

- *"Ask of me, and I will make the nations your inheritance, the ends of the earth your possession"* (Ps 2:8).

- *"Ask the Lord for rain in the springtime; it is the Lord who makes the storm clouds. He gives showers of rain to men, and plants of the field to everyone"* (Zech 10:1).

- *"And the prayer offered in faith will make the sick person well; the Lord will raise him up. If he has sinned, he will be forgiven"* (Jas 5:15).

Among the apostles, John, most completely recorded Jesus' words concerning the unlimited blessings, the measureless resources, that are ours if we correctly handle this instrument, saying; *"And I will do whatever you ask in my name, so that the Son may bring glory to the Father. You may ask me for anything in my name, and I will do it"* (Jn 14:13-14). ... *"You did not choose me, but I chose you and appointed you to go and bear fruit — fruit that will last. Then the Father will give you whatever you ask in my name"* (Jn 15:16). ...

"In that day you will no longer ask me anything. I tell you the truth, my Father will give you whatever you ask in my name. Until now you have not asked for anything in my name. Ask and you will receive, and your joy will be complete" (Jn 16:23-24). ... *"In that day you will ask in my name. I am not saying that I will ask the Father on your behalf. No, the Father himself loves you because you have loved me and have believed that I came from God"* (Jn 16:26-27).

For more on the 'Prayer of Faith", refer to the chapter on God's Precious Promises.

- ***The Prayer of Intercession*** -- This instrument is one of the more difficult instruments to play, but unquestionably, the most rewarding. Its difficulty lies in the fact that it requires more practice to become proficient in, and a far greater time commitment than many of the other instruments in the symphony of prayer. At the same time, those who take up the instrument of intercession, experience profound joy as they witness the lost responding to their prayers, marriages restored, and see unnumbered miracles take place.

  This should not be a surprise since the prophet, Isaiah, long ago said that God will not hear the prayer of a sinner (Is 59:2), but that He made intercession for the transgressor (Is 53:12).

The intercessor is encouraged to pray for everyone, and for his/her reward is promised that as a result of their prayers, we may live peaceful, quiet lives in all godliness and holiness (1 Ti 2:1-2). To intercede means to entreat on behalf of another, to stand between the accused and his accuser and plead the accused one's case on their behalf. In other words, the intercessor stands in the gap on another person's behalf. Scripture provides us with examples of some extreme, almost radical cases. Consider for instance the time when Abraham stood in the gap for his nephew, Lot, entreating God on behalf of the perverse cities of Sodom and Gomorrah.

Moses recorded this heartwarming story of two angels, together with our Lord, visiting Abraham's Bedouin dwelling, in the heat of the day, near the Oasis of Mamre. Living among the Amorites, Abram was no doubt very watchful and wary. Somehow, these three men had escaped his wary eye. Now they suddenly appeared to him as he looked up and realized that he was in the presence of his Lord! He must have sensed the importance of the visit, for he hurriedly, began to serve them, providing them rest in the shade, washing their feet, preparing and serving them the best food he had to offer.

"The Lord appeared to Abraham near the great trees of Mamre while he was sitting at the entrance to his tent in the heat of the day. Abraham looked up and saw three men standing nearby. When he saw them, he hurried from the entrance of his tent to meet them and bowed low to the ground. He said, "If I have found favor in your eyes, my lord, do not pass your servant by. Let a little water be brought, and then you may all wash your feet and rest under this tree. Let me get you something to eat, so you can be refreshed and then go on your way — now that you have come to your servant."

"Very well," they answered, "do as you say." So Abraham hurried into the tent to Sarah. "Quick!" he said, "get three seahs of fine flour and knead it and bake some bread." Then he ran to the herd and selected a choice, tender calf and gave it to a servant, who hurried to prepare it. He then brought some curds and milk and the calf that had been prepared, and set these before them. While they ate, he stood near them under a tree" (Gen 18:1-8).

When their appetite was abated, they asked Abraham about his wife, Sarah, and after determining her well-being, promised them that within the year, Sarah – now ninety, and "well past the age of childbearing" (vs 11) – would bear a son.

Sarah, who had been promised an heir for years, laughed derisively to herself, thinking: *"After I am worn out and my master is old, will I how enjoy this pleasure?"* (vs 11-12).

Revealing by his question his identity, *"the Lord said to Abraham, "Why did Sarah laugh and say, 'Will I really have a child, now that I am old?' Is anything too hard for the Lord? I **will** return to you at the appointed time next year and Sarah will have a son"* (vs 13-14).

After this exchange, *"When the men got up to leave, they looked down toward Sodom, and Abraham walked along with them to see them on their way. Then the Lord said, "Shall I hide from Abraham what I am about to do? Abraham will surely become a great and powerful nation, and all nations on earth will be blessed through him. For I have chosen him, so that he will direct his children and his household after him to keep the way of the Lord by doing what is right and just, so that the Lord will bring about for Abraham what he has promised him. Then the Lord said, "The outcry against Sodom and Gomorrah is so great and their sin so grievous that I will go down and see if what they have done is as bad as the outcry that has reached me. If not, I will know."*

Abraham's Intercession begins: *"The men turned away and went toward Sodom, but Abraham remained standing before the Lord. Then Abraham approached him and said: "Will you sweep away the righteous with the wicked? What if there are fifty righteous people in the city? Will you really sweep it away and not spare the place for the sake of the fifty righteous people in it? Far be it from you to do such a thing — to kill the righteous with the wicked, treating the righteous and the wicked alike. Far be it from you! Will not the Judge of all the earth do right?"*

"The Lord said, "If I find fifty righteous people in the city of Sodom, I will spare the whole place for their sake." Then Abraham spoke up again: "Now that I have been so bold as to speak to the Lord, though I am nothing but dust and ashes, what if the number of the righteous is five less than fifty? Will you destroy the whole city because of five people?" "If I find forty-five there," he said, "I will not destroy it." Once again he spoke to him, "What if only forty are found there?" He said, "For the sake of forty, I will not do it."

Then he said, "May the Lord not be angry, but let me speak. What if only thirty can be found there?" He answered, "I will not do it if I find thirty there." Abraham said, "Now that I have been so bold as to speak to the Lord, what if only twenty can be found there?" He said, "For the sake of twenty, I will not destroy it." Then he said, "May the Lord not be angry, but let me speak just once more. What if only ten can be found there?" He answered, "For the sake of ten, I will not destroy it." When the Lord had finished speaking with Abraham, he left, and Abraham returned home" (Gen 18:16-33).

Sadly, we know the outcome. There were not even ten righteous souls in the Jordan Plain. "Early the next morning, Abraham got up and returned to the place where he had stood before the Lord. He looked down toward Sodom and Gomorrah, toward all the land of the plain, and he saw dense smoke rising from the land, like smoke from a furnace" (Gen 19:27-28).

The cities of Sodom and Gomorrah, and the surrounding Jordan Plain were destroyed. Lot's wife -- who turned back, after the angels had set them on their way -- turned to a pillar of salt, and the entire area was so thoroughly devastated, it has been used as an example of hell fire (2 Pe 2:6; Jude 7). But, despite the outcome, consider the tenacity of Abraham, who stood in the gap for Lot and his family, and negotiated with the Lord on their behalf! Such is the role of the intercessor.

Intercession is ultimately about soul-winning -- winning the lost and redeeming the errant Christian brother or sister. God has given intercessors some powerful promises that apply specifically to their calling. Remember, "He made intercession for the transgressor" (Is 53:12). One of the most meaningful prayers of intercession for the errant brother is recorded in 1 John: "If anyone sees his brother commit a sin that does not lead to [spiritual] death, he should pray and God will give him life. I refer to those whose sin does not lead to [spiritual] death. There is a sin that leads to [such] death. I am not saying that he should pray about that" (1 John 5:16).

Jude left these encouraging words for intercessors: "Dear friends, build yourselves up in your most holy faith and **pray in the Holy Spirit**. Keep yourselves in God's love as you wait for the mercy of our Lord Jesus Christ to bring you to eternal life. **Be merciful to those who doubt; snatch others from the fire and save them; to others show mercy**, mixed with fear-hating even the clothing stained by corrupted flesh" (Jude 20-23).

The power of intercession is alluded to in the following words of Isaiah: "Justice is driven back, and righteousness stands at a distance; truth has stumbled in the streets, honesty cannot enter.

"Truth is nowhere to be found, and whoever shuns evil becomes a prey. The Lord looked and was displeased that there was no justice. When he saw that there was no one [to help] , he was appalled that there was no one to intervene (no intercessors)" (Is 59:14-16).

The Complete Jewish Bible no doubt does a better job of conveying God's response to the lack of intercessors: *"When the Lord noticed that justice had disappeared [on the earth], he became very displeased. It disgusted him even more learn that no one would do a thing about it!"* (vs 15-16).

- **The Prayer of Perseverance --** This instrument is one of greater importance than we might first imagine, since Christ took care to personally instruct his disciples in its use. Employing a parable, *"he said to them, "Suppose one of you has a friend; and you go to him in the middle of the night and say to him, 'Friend, lend me three loaves of bread, because a friend of mine who has been traveling has just arrived at my house, and I have nothing for him to eat.'*

"Now the one inside may answer, 'Don't bother me! The door is already shut, my children are with me in bed — I can't get up to give you anything!' But I tell you, even if he won't get up because the man is his friend, yet because of the man's hutzpah **(persistence or perseverance)** *he will get up and give him as much as he needs.*

"Moreover, I myself say to you: keep asking, and it will be given to you; keep seeking, and you will find; keep knocking, and the door will be opened to you. For everyone who goes on asking receives; and he who goes on seeking finds; and to him who continues knocking, the door will be opened"* (Lk 11:5-10 CJB).

The use of this instrument differs from the prayer of petition in that we have been encouraged -- by Christ himself -- to keep asking, keep seeking, and keep knocking. In other words, we are instructed to keep on keeping on, until our petition is granted, our prayer answered. We find an example of this instrument being played proficiently in Acts 12. *"It was about this time that King Herod arrested some who belonged to the church, intending to persecute them. He had James, the brother of John, put to death with the sword. When he saw that this pleased the Jews, he proceeded to seize Peter also. This happened during the Feast of Unleavened Bread.*

"After arresting him, he put him in prison, handing him over to be guarded by four squads of four soldiers each. Herod intended to bring him out for public trial after the Passover. So Peter was kept in prison, but the church was earnestly praying to God for him.

"The night before Herod was to bring him to trial, Peter was sleeping between two soldiers, bound with two chains, and sentries stood guard at the entrance. Suddenly an angel of the Lord appeared and a light shone in the cell. He struck Peter on the side and woke him up. "Quick, get up!" he said, and the chains fell off Peter's wrists.

"Then the angel said to him, "Put on your clothes and sandals." And Peter did so. "Wrap your cloak around you and follow me," the angel told him. Peter followed him out of the prison, but he had no idea that what the angel was doing was really happening; he thought he was seeing a vision. They passed the first and second guards and came to the iron gate leading to the city. It opened for them by itself, and they went through it. When they had walked the length of one street, suddenly the angel left him" (Acts 12:1-10).

Not only did the Lord respond to the prayers of the church by releasing Peter from prison, Herod's pride and persecution of the church cost him the ultimate price. *"In the morning (following Peter's escape), there was no small commotion among the soldiers as to what had become of Peter. After Herod had a thorough search made for him and did not find him, he cross-examined the guards and ordered that they be executed.*

"Then Herod went from Judea to Caesarea and stayed there a while. He had been quarreling with the people of Tyre and Sidon; they now joined together and sought an audience with him. Having secured the support of Blastus, a trusted personal servant of the king, they asked for peace, because they depended on the king's country for their food supply. On the appointed day Herod, wearing his royal robes, sat on his throne and delivered a public address to the people. They shouted, "This is the voice of a god, not of a man." Immediately, because Herod did not give praise to God, an angel of the Lord struck him down, and he was eaten by worms and died" (Acts 12:18-23).

What brought about the release of Peter from prison, where he was being held for public execution; and the demise of Herod, the nemesis of the church? The persistent, prevailing, prayer of the church! When the church believes she is in the right -- following God's will, fulfilling His mission for them -- there is only one way she can lose, by giving up.

Another example of the prayer of persistence at work is found in the book of Daniel. Daniel had seen a vision of a great battle that so touched him he mourned -- praying and fasting for three weeks. Then -- suddenly -- his prayer was answered.

"On the twenty-fourth day of the first month, as I was standing on the bank of the great river, the Tigris, I looked up and there before me was a man dressed in linen, with a belt of the finest gold around his waist. His body was like chrysolite, his face like lightning, his eyes like flaming torches, his arms and legs like the gleam of burnished bronze, and his voice like the sound of a multitude. I, Daniel, was the only one who saw the vision; the men with me did not see it, but such terror overwhelmed them that they fled and hid themselves. So I was left alone, gazing at this great vision; I had no strength left, my face turned deathly pale and I was helpless. Then I heard him speaking, and as I listened to him, I fell into a deep sleep, my face to the ground.

"A hand touched me and set me trembling on my hands and knees. He said, "Daniel, you who are highly esteemed, consider carefully the words I am about to speak to you, and stand up, for I have now been sent to you." And when he said this to me, I stood up trembling" (Dan 10:4-11). What an experience! Yet, I can imagine Daniel thinking -- "If I'm so highly esteemed, how come it's taken you twenty-one days to respond to my plight?

"Then the angel continued, "Do not be afraid, Daniel. Since the first day that you set your mind to gain understanding and to humble yourself before your God, your words were heard, and I have come in response to them. But the prince of the Persian kingdom resisted me twenty-one days. Then Michael, one of the chief princes, came to help me, because I was detained there with the king of Persia" (Dan 10:12-14).

What if Daniel had given up after a week, or after two weeks, or after twenty days? How many times, because you cannot see what is happening in the spirit realm, have you given up, when in fact, God has dispatched an angel with the answer to your prayer? How many spiritual battles have been lost, how many souls doomed, because we -- the church -- has given up, thinking God isn't listening to our prayers; when in fact, Michael and his angels and Satan and his are squaring off in the unseen realm of the spirit world.

Little do we realize that when we give up, the angels warring on our behalf, and endeavoring to deliver God's promised blessings, are dismissed -- not by God, but by us.

After all: *"Are not **all angels ministering spirits sent to serve** those who will inherit salvation?"* (Heb 1:14). When we quit praying, their commission to serve is suspended. This battle in the unseen is referenced in the writings of the apostle, Paul, who in his letter to the Colossians, mentions the need for persistence, writing: *"All over the world this gospel is bearing fruit and growing, just as it has been doing among you since the day you heard it and understood God's grace in all its truth. You learned it from Epaphras, our dear fellow servant, who is a faithful minister of Christ on our behalf, and who also told us of your love in the Spirit. For this reason, since the day we heard about you, we have not stopped praying for you and asking God to fill you with the knowledge of his will through all spiritual wisdom and understanding"* (Col 1:6-9).

The need for this type of persistence is further highlighted in his letter to the Thessolonians. *"But, brothers, when we were torn away from you for a short time (in person, not in thought), **out of our intense longing we made every effort to see you**. For we wanted to come to you — certainly I, Paul, did, **again and again — but Satan stopped us**"* (1 Th 2:17-19).

These illustrations certainly validate Paul's words concerning spiritual warfare in Ephesians. *"Put on the full armor of God so that you can take your stand against the devil's schemes. For our struggle is not against flesh and blood, but against the rulers, against the authorities, against the powers of this dark world and against the spiritual forces of evil in the heavenly realms"* (Eph 6:11-12).

The Prayer of Praise and Thanksgiving -- This instrument, according to the model prayer Christ gave his disciples -- the Lord's Prayer -- these instruments are those that should begin each symphonic presentation -- praising God for His Majesty, His Divine Attributes and Glory; and for His unconditional commitment and unfathomable love extended toward us. David wrote:

• *"Great is the Lord, and most worthy of praise"* (Ps 48:1). Consider some of His attributes -- all worthy of our praise:

• *"Praise the greatness of our God! He is our Rock, his works are perfect, and all his ways are just. A faithful God who does no wrong, upright and just is He"* (Dt 32:3-4).

• *"Praise the Lord who rescues us"* (Ex 18:10).

• *"Praise the Lord, for He performs awesome wonders"* (Dt 10:21).

97

- *"Praise the Lord, who will uphold our righteous cause"* (1 Sa 25:39).

- *"Praise the Lord, who saves us from our enemies"* (2 Sa 22:4).

- *"Praise the Lord, who fulfills His promises"* (1 Ki 8:56; 2 Ch 6:4).

- *"Praise the Lord, whose love endures forever"* (2 Ch 20:21).

- *"Praise the Lord, who counsels us, even while we sleep"* (Ps 16:7).

- *"Praise the Lord, who is from everlasting to everlasting"* (Ps 41:13).

- *"Praise the Lord, who is our strength, our shield, and fortress"* (Ps 59:17).

- *"Praise the Lord, who neither rejects our prayer, nor withholds His love from us"* (Ps 66:20).

- *"Praise the Lord, He defends the widows and fathers the fatherless"* (Ps 68:5).

- *"Praise the Lord, who daily bears our burdens"* (Ps 68:19).

- *"Praise the Lord for His faithfulness"* (Ps 71:22).

- *"Praise the Lord, who redeems us (buying us back from Satan, with his own blood!"* (Ps 71:23).

- *"Praise the Lord, who saves us"* (Ps 96:2).

- *"Praise the Lord for He is just"* (Ps 101:1).

- *"Praise the Lord, who forgives all our sins, heals all our diseases, redeems us from the pit of hell, crowns us with love and compassion, and satisfies our desires"* (Ps 102:3-5).

- *"Praise the Lord, that in him we might enjoy the prosperity of His chosen ones"* (Ps 106:5).

- *"Praise the Lord, who is the beginning of wisdom"* (Ps 106:5).

- *"Praise the Lord, who opens the wombs of the barren"* (Ps 113:9)

- *"Praise the Lord who has fearfully and wonderfully made us"* (Ps 139:14).

- *"Praise the Lord, who trains us for warfare – spiritual warfare"* (Ps 144:1).

- *"Praise the Lord, who rescues the needy from the hands of the wicked"* (Jer 20:13).

- *"Praise the Lord, who has given us, in Christ, every spiritual blessing"* (Eph 1:3).

  Praise and thanksgiving are to be vocalized – preferably with instrumental accompaniment. We *"enter his gates with thanksgiving and his courts with praise"* (Ps 100:4). Our entrance is to be joyful and festive: *"Let them praise his name with dancing and make music to him with tambourine and harp. For the Lord takes delight in his people"* (Ps 149:3-4).

- **The prayer of Supplication** -- This instrument is called for when one has a need, but does not know for sure, what God's will is in the matter. In these instances, we can come before the throne of grace and entreat the Lord, appealing to His mercy and grace. *"Do not be anxious about anything, but in everything [be confident], by prayer and petition, with thanksgiving, present your requests to God. And the peace of God, which transcends all understanding, will guard your hearts and your minds in Christ Jesus"* (Phil 4:6-7).

- **The prayer of Worship** -- This instrument, unlike the others, is not something vocalized: it is, rather, an attitude of the heart. God seeks true worshipers, who worship in spirit and truth. Jesus said: *"a time is coming and has now come when the true worshipers will worship the Father in spirit and truth, for they are the kind of worshipers the Father seeks. God is spirit, and his worshipers must worship in spirit and in truth"* (Jn 4:23-24). The proper attitude of heart is expressed in the beatitudes: Blessed are the humble, who mourn over sin in the church, are meek, who hunger and thirst after righteousness, are merciful, pure in heart, and peacemakers (Mt 5:3-12). Worshipers are generally joyful people (Lk 24:52). Filled with the Spirit, worshippers often exercise the spiritual gifts of discernment and prophecy (Acts 13:2).

- **Summary** -- There is one critical flaw in the metaphor employed -- that of comparing the various types of prayer to a symphony. In a symphonic musical production, each instrument is played by a different individual, gifted in its use and place in the overall musical production.

The difference between this and a symphony of prayer is that each and every Christian is instructed to *"**pray in the Spirit and on all occasions with all kinds of prayers and requests**"* (Eph 6:18).

This might at first seem impossible. However, reflecting on what we learned in chapter 1, that our DNA actually sings, that born-again Christians sing a new song unto the Lord (Ps 96:1; Rev 5:9; 14:3), and that our own tabrets and pipes (Ezek 28:13), present a symphony of praise unto the Lord, the metaphor comes together.

Finally, we are to *"Pray without ceasing. In every thing give thanks: for this is the will of God in Christ Jesus concerning you. Quench not the Spirit. Despise not prophesying. Prove all things; hold fast that which is good"* (1 Th 5:17-21).

Personal Application:
Take a few moments to reflect on your familiarity with, and competency in the use of, each type of prayer that comprises the symphony of prayer, mentioned in this chapter.

Ex.	V.G.	Good	Fair	N. I.	Type of Prayer		
[ ]	[ ]	[ ]	[ ]	[ ]	The	Prayer of	Agreement
[ ]	[ ]	[ ]	[ ]	[ ]	The	Prayer of	Blessing
[ ]	[ ]	[ ]	[ ]	[ ]	The	Prayer of	Cursing
[ ]	[ ]	[ ]	[ ]	[ ]	The	Prayer of	Command
[ ]	[ ]	[ ]	[ ]	[ ]	The	Prayer of	Commitment
[ ]	[ ]	[ ]	[ ]	[ ]	The	Prayer of	Consecration
[ ]	[ ]	[ ]	[ ]	[ ]	The	Prayer of	Declaration
[ ]	[ ]	[ ]	[ ]	[ ]	The	Prayer of	Dedication
[ ]	[ ]	[ ]	[ ]	[ ]	The	Prayer of	Faith/Reception
[ ]	[ ]	[ ]	[ ]	[ ]	The	Prayer of	Intercession
[ ]	[ ]	[ ]	[ ]	[ ]	The	Prayer of	Perseverance
[ ]	[ ]	[ ]	[ ]	[ ]	The	Prayer of	Praise & Thanks
[ ]	[ ]	[ ]	[ ]	[ ]	The	Prayer of	Supplication
[ ]	[ ]	[ ]	[ ]	[ ]	The	Prayer of	Worship

Ex. = excellent; V.G. = very good, and N.I. = needs improvement

Which type are you most familiar with?_____

Which type are you least familiar with? _____

Which type do you engage in most? _____

Which type do you engage in least? _____

As a Spiritual Warrior, which type do you believe God has called

you to engage in? _____

How much time a day do you spend in focused prayer?

_____

Do you believe that this amount of time is:

[ ] Not enough; [ ] About right [ ] Too much

If other than 'about right', are you willing to make a commitment to correct this?

[ ] Yes,   [ ] No

If no, what is your reason? _____

Chapter Six ~ Living on God's Promises

"He has given us his very great and precious promises, so that through them you may participate in the divine nature and escape the corruption in the world caused by evil desires" (2 Pe 1:4).

God's Promises and The Law:

The importance of our learning to rely on God's Promises, rather than our legalistically enforcing God's law, is highlighted in the preceding and following Scriptures:

- *"Is the law, therefore, opposed to the promises of God? Absolutely not! For if a law had been given that could impart life, then righteousness would certainly have come by the law. But the Scripture declares that the whole world is a prisoner of sin, so that what was promised, being given through faith in Jesus Christ, might be given to those who believe.*

- *"Before this faith came, we were held prisoners by the law, locked up until faith should be revealed. So the law was put in charge to lead us to Christ that we might be justified by faith. Now that faith has come, we are no longer under the supervision of the law. You are all sons of God through faith in Christ Jesus, for all of you who were baptized into Christ have clothed yourselves with Christ"* (Gal 3:21-27).

- *"Your promises have been thoroughly tested, and your servant loves them"* (Ps 119:140).

- *"You know with all your heart and soul that **not one of all the good promises the Lord your God gave you has failed**. Every promise has been fulfilled; not one has failed"* (Jos 23:14).

- *"The Lord is faithful to all his promises and loving toward all he has made"* (Ps 145:13).

- *"**For no matter how many promises God has made, they are "Yes" in Christ**"* (2 Cor 1:20).

- *"Then they believed his promises and sang his praise"* (Ps 106:12).

- *"My eyes stay open through the watches of the night, that I may meditate on your promises"* (Ps 119:148).

God's Promises & Healing ~ Body, soul & Spirit:
In the symbolism of the Genesis story of creation, the Tree of Life (the Family of God) straddles the River of the Water of Life. The symbolism of the 'river of the water of life' is reminiscent of Jesus' words, spoken long ago to a Samaritan woman, who came to draw water from the well where Jesus was waiting.

Jesus said to her, *"Will you give me a drink?" (His disciples had gone into the town to buy food.) The Samaritan woman said to him, "You are a Jew and I am a Samaritan woman. How can you ask me for a drink?" (For Jews do not associate with Samaritans.) Jesus answered her, "If you knew the gift of God and who it is that asks you for a drink, you would have asked him and he would have given you living water."*

"Sir," the woman said, *"you have nothing to draw with and the well is deep. **Where can you get this living water**? Are you greater than our father Jacob, who gave us the well and drank from it himself, as did also his sons and his flocks and herds?" Jesus answered, "**Everyone who drinks this water will be thirsty again, but whoever drinks the water I give him will never thirst. Indeed, the water I give him will become in him a spring of water welling up to eternal life**"* (John 4:7-14). Water also represents multitudes of peoples. *"Then the angel said to me, "The waters you saw, where the prostitute sits, are peoples, multitudes, nations and languages"* (Rev 17:15).

The Tree of Life:
The Tree of Life is described in Scripture as being rooted, or standing, on both sides of the River of Life, representing the redeemed Family of God that spans all people groups. The universality of God's family is further symbolized by the fact that the Tree of Life bears 12 crops of fruit, each one different, yielding a different fruit each month. The 12 crops of fruit and the 12 months, both representing the number of completion (i.e., the 12 Patriarchs, the 12 Apostles, the 12 gates into the Holy City, the 12 Sacred Stones in the foundation of the walls of the Holy City, etc.). The leaves of the Tree of Life are, in the text under consideration, *'for the healing of the nations'*. The leaves of the tree of life are also identified elsewhere as the promises of God, a concept consistent with what Peter says in our key text for this chapter:

*"**For His divine power has bestowed upon us all things that [are requisite and suited] to life and godliness,** through the [full, personal] knowledge of Him Who called us by and to His own glory and excellence (virtue). **By means of these He has bestowed on us His precious and exceedingly great promises, so that through them you may escape [by flight] from the moral decay (rottenness and corruption) that is in the world because of covetousness (lust and greed), and become sharers (partakers) of the divine nature."* Continuing, Peter admonishes: *"For this very reason, **adding your diligence [to the divine promises],** employ every effort in exercising your faith to develop virtue (excellence, resolution, Christian energy), and in [exercising] virtue [develop] knowledge (intelligence), And in [exercising] knowledge [develop] self-control, and in [exercising] self-control [develop] steadfastness (patience, endurance), and in [exercising] steadfastness [develop] godliness (piety), And in [exercising] godliness [develop] brotherly affection, and in [exercising] brotherly affection [develop] Christian love.*

*"For as these qualities are yours and increasingly abound in you, they will keep [you] from being idle or unfruitful unto the [full personal] knowledge of our Lord Jesus Christ (the Messiah, the Anointed One). For whoever lacks these qualities is blind, [spiritually] shortsighted, seeing only what is near to him, and has become oblivious [to the fact] that he was cleansed from his old sins. Because of this, brethren, be all the more solicitous and eager to make sure (to ratify, to strengthen, to make steadfast) your calling and election; for **if you do this, you will never stumble or fall. Thus there will be richly and abundantly provided for you entry into the eternal kingdom of our Lord and Savior Jesus Christ"*** (2 Peter 1:3-11).

Basic Principles for claiming God's promises:
These principles introduced earlier are these:

1. **A**sk

2. **B**elieve

3. **C**laim

Ask ~ Asking according to God's expressed will.

* *"And I will do whatever you **ask** in my name, so that the Son may bring glory to the Father. You may **ask** me for anything in my name, and I will do it"* (Jn 14:13-14).

* *"If you remain in me and my words remain in you, **ask** whatever you wish, and it will be given you"* (Jn 15:7).

* *"You did not choose me, but I chose you and appointed you to go and bear fruit — fruit that will last. Then the Father will give you whatever you **ask** in my name"* (Jn 15:16).

* *"In that day you will no longer **ask** me anything. I tell you the truth, my Father will give you whatever you **ask** in my name. Until now you have not asked for anything in my name. **Ask** and you will receive, and your joy will be complete"* (Jn 16:23-24).

* *"In that day you will **ask** in my name. I am not saying that I will ask the Father on your behalf"* (Jn 16:26).

* *"Now to him who is able to do immeasurably more than all we **ask** or imagine, according to his power that is at work within us, to him be glory in the church and in Christ Jesus throughout all generations, for ever and ever! Amen"* (Eph 3:20-21).

* *"You want something but don't get it. You kill and covet, but you cannot have what you want. You quarrel and fight. You do not have, because you do not **ask** God"* (Jas 4:2).

* *"Dear friends, if our hearts do not condemn us, we have confidence before God and receive from him anything we **ask**, because we obey his commands and do what pleases him"* (1 Jn 3:21-22),

* *"This is the confidence we have in approaching God: that if*

we **ask** anything according to his will, he hears us. And if we know that he hears us — whatever we ask — we know that we have what we asked of him" (1 Jn 5:14-15).

Believe ~ Believe unquestionably in God's Word

- "If you **believe**, you will receive whatever you ask for in prayer" (Mt 21:22).

- "Therefore I tell you, whatever you ask for in prayer, **believe** that you have received it, and it will be yours" (Mk 11:24).

- "Jesus cried out, "When a man **believes** in me, he does not **believe** in me only, but in the one who sent me. When he looks at me" (Jn 12:44-45).

- "His incomparably great power for us who **believe**. That power is like the working of his mighty strength, which he exerted in Christ when he raised him from the dead" (Eph 1:19-20).

- "But when he asks, he must **believe and not doubt**, because he who doubts is like a wave of the sea, blown and tossed by the wind. That man should not think he will receive anything from the Lord" (Jas 1:6-7).

Claim ~ Crying out to God for His intervention, and giving Him thanks, that according to His promise, you have received His promised gift.

- "I tell you, whatever you ask for in prayer, **believe that you have received it,** and it will be yours" (Mk 11:24).

- "It was not through law that Abraham and his offspring received the promise that he would be heir of the world, but through the righteousness that comes by faith" (Ro 4:13).

- "Do not be anxious about anything, but in everything, **by prayer and petition, with thanksgiving, present your requests to God**" (Php 4:6).

- "You will be made rich in every way so that you can be generous on every occasion, and through us your generosity will result in thanksgiving to God" (2 Co 9:11).

107

- *"With praise and thanksgiving they sang to the Lord: "He is good; his love to Israel endures forever"* (Ezr 3:11).

- *"He who sacrifices thank offerings honors me, and he prepares the way so that I may show him the salvation of God"* (Ps 50:23).

- *"If you cry out to me, I will certainly hear your cry"* (Ex 22:23).

- *"When we cried out to the Lord, he heard our cry and sent an angel and brought us out of Egypt"* (Nu 20:16).

- *"We will cry out to you in our distress, and you will hear us and save us"* (2 Ch 20:9).

- *"The righteous cry out, and the Lord hears them; he delivers them from all their troubles"* (Ps 34:17).

Other Conditions for realizing the benefits of God's Covenant Promises, include:

Obedience ~

- *"If you **obey** me fully and keep my covenant, then out of all nations you will be my treasured possession. Although the whole earth is mine, you will be for me a kingdom of priests and a holy nation"* (Ex 19:5-6).

- *"The Lord commanded us to **obey** all these decrees and to fear the Lord our God, so that we might always prosper and be kept alive"* (Dt 6:24).

- *"Be careful to **obey** all these regulations I am giving you, so that it may always go well with you and your children after you, because you will be doing what is good and right in the eyes of the Lord your God"* (Dt 12:28).

- *"If you fully **obey** the Lord your God and carefully follow all his commands I give you today, the Lord your God will set you high above all the nations on earth. All these blessings will come upon you and accompany you if you obey the Lord your God"* (Dt 28:1-2).

- *"If they **obey** and serve Him, they will spend the rest of their days in prosperity and their years in contentment"* (Job 36:11).

- *"Blessed rather are those who hear the word of God and **obey** it"* (Lk 11:28).

• *"And we receive from him anything we ask, because we* **obey** *his commands and do what pleases him"* (1 Jn 3:22).

Persevere ~

• *"You need to* **persevere** *so that when you have done the will of God, you will receive what he has promised"* (Heb 10:36).

• *"Whoever does not* **persevere** *and carry his own cross and come after (follow) Me cannot be My disciple"* (Lk 14:27).

• *"Be steadfast and* **persevere***!"* (1 Pe 5:12).

• *"Look to yourselves (take care) that you may not lose (throw away or destroy) all that we and you have labored for, but that you may [* **persevere** *until you] win and receive back a perfect reward [in full].* (2 Jn 8).

• *"If we* **persevere***, we will also rule with him If we disown him, he will also disown us"* (2 Ti 2:12 CJB).

• *"He is always wrestling in prayer for you, that you may* **stand firm** *in all the will of God, mature and fully assured"* (Col 4:12).

Pray According to God's Expressed Will ~

• *"This is the confidence we have in approaching God: that if we* **ask anything according to his will***, he hears us. And if we know that he hears us — whatever we ask — we know that we have what we asked of him"* (1 Jn 5:14-15).

Consistency ~

• *"Never be lacking in zeal, but* **keep your spiritual fervor***, serving the Lord. Be joyful in hope, patient in affliction, faithful in prayer"* (Ro 12:11-12).

Avoid Anger & Disputes ~

• *"I want men everywhere to lift up holy hands in prayer,* **without anger or disputing***"* (1 Ti 2:8).

• *"He that is* **slow to anger** *is better than the mighty"* (Pr 16:32).

• *"Everyone should be quick to listen, slow to speak and* **slow to become angry***, for a man's anger does not bring about the righteous life that God desires"* (Jas 1:19).

Escape Lust ~

- *"Ye lust, and have not: ye kill, and desire to have, and cannot obtain: ye fight and war, yet ye have not, because ye ask not. **Ye ask, and receive not, because ye ask amiss, that ye may consume it upon your lusts**"* (Jas 4:2-3).

- *"**Put to death**, therefore, whatever belongs to your earthly nature: sexual immorality, impurity, **lust**, evil desires and greed, which is idolatry"* (Col 3:5).

- *"When tempted, no one should say, "God is tempting me." For God cannot be tempted by evil, nor does he tempt anyone; but each one is tempted when, by his own evil desire, he is dragged away and enticed. Then, after desire has conceived, it gives birth to sin; and sin, when it is full-grown, gives birth to death"* (Jas 1:13-15).

- *"There hath no temptation taken you but such as is common to man: but God is faithful, who will not suffer you to be tempted above that ye are able; but will with the temptation also make a way to escape, that ye may be able to bear it"* (1 Co 10:13).

Hindrances to the Prayer of Faith constituting additional conditions:

Unconfessed sin ~

- *"If I regard wickedness in my heart, The Lord will not hear me"* (Ps 66:18).

- *"If our hearts do not condemn us, we have confidence before God and receive from him anything we ask"* (1 Jn 3:21-22).

Unforgiveness ~

- *"When you stand praying, if you hold anything against anyone, forgive him, so that your Father in heaven may forgive you your sins"* (Mk 11:25).

Mistreatment of One's Spouse ~

- *"Husbands, in the same way be considerate as you live with your wives, and treat them with respect as the weaker partner and as heirs with you of the gracious gift of life, so that nothing will hinder your prayers"* (1 Pet. 3:7).

Neglecting the Poor and Needy ~

- *"If a man shuts his ears to the cry of the poor, he too will cry out and not be answered"* (Prov. 21:13).

- *"Don't withhold good from those to whom it is due, When it is in the power of your hand to do it. Don't say to your neighbor, "Go, and come again, Tomorrow I will give it to you," When you have it by you." (Pro 3:27,28).*

- *"If you do not listen to the cry of the poor, God will not listen to your prayers" (Lk 6:38).*

Selfishness ~
- *"You ask and do not receive, because you ask amiss, that you may spend it on your pleasures" (James 4:3).*

Double-mindedness ~
- *"But when he asks, he must believe and not doubt, because he who doubts is like a wave of the sea, blown and tossed by the wind. That man should not think he will receive anything from the Lord; he is a double-minded man, unstable in all he does" (Jas 1:6-8).*

Spiritual Indifference ~

- *"One who turns away his ear from hearing the law, even his prayer shall be an abomination" (Pro 28:9).*

- *"If ... My words abide in you, you well ask what you desire, and it will be done for you" (John 15:7).*

Self-righteousness ~
- *"Everyone who exalts himself will be humbled, and he who humbles himself will be exalted" (Lk 18:14).*

Hardness of Heart ~

- *"He that turneth away his ear from hearing the law, even his prayer shall be abomination" (Pro 28:9).*

Failure to resist Satan ~

- *"**Resist the devil**, and he will flee from you" (Jas 4:7).*

- *"Finally, be strong in the Lord, and in the strength of his might. Put on the whole armor of God, that you may be able to **stand against the wiles of the devil**. For our wrestling is not against flesh and blood, but against the principalities, against the powers, against the world's rulers of the darkness of this age, and against the spiritual hosts of wickedness in the heavenly places. Therefore, put on the whole armor of God, that you may be able to withstand in the evil day, and, having done all, to stand" (Eph 6:10-13).*

- **"Be sober and self-controlled**. Be watchful. Your adversary the devil, walks around like a roaring lion, seeking whom he may devour. **Withstand him** steadfast in your faith, knowing that your brothers who are in the world are undergoing the same sufferings" (1 Pe 5:8,9).

Idolatry ~

- "What am I saying then? That a thing sacrificed to idols is anything, or that an idol is anything? But I say that the things which the Gentiles sacrifice, they sacrifice to demons, and not to God, and I don't desire that you would have communion with demons. You can't both drink the cup of the Lord and the cup of demons. **You can't both partake of the table of the Lord, and of the table of demons**. Or do we provoke the Lord to jealousy? Are we stronger than he?" (1 Cor 10:19-22).

- **"Don't be unequally yoked with unbelievers**, for what fellowship have righteousness and iniquity? Or what communion has light with darkness? What agreement has Christ with Belial? Or what portion has a believer with an unbeliever? **What agreement has a temple of God with idols? For you are a temple of the living God**. Even as God said, "I will dwell in them, and walk in them; and I will be their God, and they will be my people." Therefore, "'Come out from among them, And be separate,' says the Lord, 'Touch no unclean thing. I will receive you. I will be to you a Father. You will be to me sons and daughters,' says the Lord Almighty" (2 Cor 6:14-18).

  [Attempts to find healing by use of New Age medication, charms, folklore superstitions, witchcraft medicines, pilgrimages to holy places, will make God jealous and He will not listen to your prayers. God may make use of medicine and medical advances, but He expects these to be used with liberal amounts of prayer to your heavenly Father. You should find what God's will is in your illness and also call the Elders of the Assembly to lay hands on you when you are ill.]

- "Is any among you sick? Let him call for the elders of the assembly, and let them pray over him, anointing him with oil in the name of the Lord, and the prayer of faith will heal him who is sick, and the Lord will raise him up. If he has committed sins, he will be forgiven. Confess your offenses to one another, and pray one for another, that you may be healed. The effective, earnest prayer of a righteous man is powerfully effective." (Jas 5:14-16).

Impatience ~

If we do not receive an answer the first time we ask, we should pray again. And if we do not have an answer the hundredth time, we should go on praying until we get an answer. If we request something and stop praying, forgetting what we asked for, God will also forget and not answer our request. The women who asked Jesus to heal her daughter would not give up until her plea was answered. When Daniel prayed for understanding, God sent a messenger the same day, who was hindered and arrived twenty one days later. If Daniel had given up before the messenger arrived his prayer would never have been answered.

- *"Let us not grow weary but be constant in prayer"* (Lk 11:5-13; 18:1-8).

Failure to fulfill our Covenant Responsibilities ~

- One cannot sincerely pray, *"Your kingdom come"* unless they are doing what God desires them to do to hasten the coming of His kingdom.

- As a servant of our Lord, one cannot say, *"Lord, do this or that."* Servants say, *"Lord, what do you want me to do?"* The satisfaction of a servant is to see his Lord satisfied. One may see a work that someone else is doing and desire to do the same, but it is not theirs to do unless, or until, God assigns that work to them.

- *"Not everyone who says to me, 'Lord, Lord,' will enter into the Kingdom of Heaven; but he who does the will of my Father who is in heaven. Many will tell me in that day, 'Lord, Lord, didn't we prophesy in your name, in your name cast out demons, and in your name do many mighty works?' Then I will tell them, 'I never knew you. Depart from me, you who work iniquity.'"* (Mt 7:21-23).

- *"But who is there among you, having a servant plowing or keeping sheep, that will say, when he comes in from the field, 'Come immediately and sit down at the table,' and will not rather tell him, 'Prepare my supper, clothe yourself properly, and serve me, while I eat and drink. Afterward you shall eat and drink'? Does he thank that servant because he did the things that were commanded? I think not. Even so you also, when you have done all the things that are commanded you, say, 'We are unworthy servants. We have done our duty.'"* (Lk 17:7-10).

- *"He who loves his life will lose it. He who hates his life in this world will keep it to eternal life. {12:26} If anyone serves me, let him follow me. Where I am, there will my servant also be. If anyone serves me, the Father will honor him."* (Jn 12:25,26).

- *"Therefore, my beloved brothers, be steadfast, immovable, always abounding in the Lord's work, because you know that your labor is not in vain in the Lord."* (1 Cor 15:58).

- *"Having gifts differing according to the grace that was given to us, if prophecy, let us prophesy according to the proportion of our faith; or service, let us give ourselves to service; or he who teaches, to his teaching; or he who exhorts, to his exhorting: he who gives, let him do it with liberality; he who rules, with diligence; he who shows mercy, with cheerfulness."* (Rom 12:6-8).

Vain repetition ~

- *"In praying, don't use vain repetitions, as the Gentiles do; for they think that they will be heard for their much speaking. Therefore don't be like them, for your Father knows what things you need, before you ask him"* (Mt 6:7,8).

Believing God is Obligated to grant one's request ~

- Some Christians believe that God is obligated to answer their prayers because they are faithful in attendance, tithing, Bible reading, praying, and doing good. Doing all these things does not obligate God to answer us. Our works do not give us a claim on God that He must provide our needs or give us all the things on our "want list."

- Our prayers are answered because of our relationship with Jesus. Only when we are in Him and He in us can we approach God with our requests and expect answers. Our attitude should be the same as Habakkuk's, who said he would rejoice in the Lord regardless of what happened.

- *"Though the fig tree does not bud and there are no grapes on the vines, though the olive crop fails and the fields produce no food, though there are no sheep in the pen and no cattle in the stalls, yet I will rejoice in the Lord, I will be joyful in God my Savior"* (Hab 3:17-18).

- *"My God, turn your ear, and hear; open your eyes, and see our desolations, and the city which is called by your name: for we do not present our petitions before you for our righteousness, but for your great mercies' sake. Lord, hear; Lord, forgive; Lord, listen and do; don't defer, for your own sake, my God, because your city and your people are called by your name."* (Dan 9:18,19).

Failing to Pray in Jesus' Name [Logos] ~

Properly understood, removing this hindrance to answered prayer, essentially removes all the others, fulfills all the conditions and meets all the principles of the prayer of faith.

The night Jesus was arrested and taken to Caiaphas, the High Priest, He spent considerable time instructing the disciples. Seven times He told them to pray in His name. Praying in the name of Jesus means that you have been given the power and authority of Jesus to do the work of God. All authority has been given to Jesus, which in turn has been made available to us. Therefore there is no excuse for the church not accomplishing the work of God. Whatever task God has assigned you, you can do in the authority of the name of Jesus.

In baptism, you were buried with Christ – in the name of Jesus. Demons are cast out in the name of Jesus. Peter healed the lame man in the name of Jesus. The authority and power in Jesus name has not changed. The authority is still there in His Name. So, today you can do the same in the name of Jesus.

However, just adding the words, "In the name of Jesus" at the end of your prayers does not guarantee that your prayers will be answered. The word 'name' used in the texts referenced in John, is the Greek word 'logos,' not the Greek word 'onoma' normally used to identify one's given name. In contrast, the word, logos, refers to the essence of all that one is -- the nature and character of one. To pray "in the name of Jesus" means you are making your request to God in the authority of His Son to whom all authority has been given. Jesus only gives this authority to those who know the will of God; pray and act accordingly.

Your will must be in complete harmony with the will of the Father. God's will is that you become like His Son. When you remain in Jesus and His words remain in you, you will know His will. Then, you can ask whatever you wish and it will be given you. You cannot seek wealth, health, prosperity, success, ease, comfort, spirituality, or fruitfulness for your own enjoyment, advancement, or prosperity.

Scripture is clear on this point. *"You desire things and don't have them. You kill, and you are jealous, and you still can't get them. So you fight and quarrel.* **The reason you don't have is that you don't pray! Or you pray and don't receive, because you pray with the wrong motive, that of wanting to indulge your own desires**" (James 4:2-3 CJB).

Prayers that are answered are those that bring glory to the Father. (See Jn 14:13,14; 15:16; 16:23,24.).

To illustrate the principle of 'praying in his name,' Jesus related the following parable:

"Two men went up into the temple to pray; one was a Pharisee, and the other was a tax collector. The Pharisee stood and prayed to himself like this: 'God, I thank you, that I am not like the rest of men, extortioners, unrighteous, adulterers, or even like this tax collector. I fast twice a week. I give tithes of all that I get.' But the tax collector, standing far away, wouldn't even lift up his eyes to heaven, but beat his breast, saying, 'God, be merciful to me, a sinner!' I tell you, this man went down to his house justified rather than the other; for everyone who exalts himself will be humbled, but he who humbles himself will be exalted" (Lk 18:10-14).

To familiarize yourself with God's promises, we recommend that you add to your weaponry as a spiritual warrior, one or more of the following books:

- God's Precious Promises, J.V. & P.M. Potter, Advocare, 2010.
- All the Promises of the Bible, H. Lockyer, Zondervan, 1990.
- The Bible Promise Book, Barbour Books, 1899.
- Bible Promises for You, Inspiro, 2005
- God's Promises for Every Day, Thomas Nelson, 1996.
- God's Promises for Your Every Need, Thomas Nelson, 1995
- The Complete Personalized Promise Bible, Harrison House, 2004.

Personal Application:

1. What provision has God provided to enable us to participate in

   His Divine Nature? _____

2. Can one live under the law and live according to God's promises at the same time?

3. What can cause God's promises to fail? _____

4. Identify the basic principles for claiming God's promises: _____

Ex.	V.G.	Good	Fair	N.I.	Condition
[ ]	[ ]	[ ]	[ ]	[ ]	Obedience
[ ]	[ ]	[ ]	[ ]	[ ]	Perseverance
[ ]	[ ]	[ ]	[ ]	[ ]	Praying God's Expressed Will
[ ]	[ ]	[ ]	[ ]	[ ]	Consistency in Prayer
[ ]	[ ]	[ ]	[ ]	[ ]	Avoiding Anger & Disputes
[ ]	[ ]	[ ]	[ ]	[ ]	Escaping Lust
[ ]	[ ]	[ ]	[ ]	[ ]	Resolving Unconfessed Sin
[ ]	[ ]	[ ]	[ ]	[ ]	Walking in Forgiveness
[ ]	[ ]	[ ]	[ ]	[ ]	Treating Spouse Righteously
[ ]	[ ]	[ ]	[ ]	[ ]	Compassion for Poor & Needy
[ ]	[ ]	[ ]	[ ]	[ ]	Other-centered vs Selfishness
[ ]	[ ]	[ ]	[ ]	[ ]	Not Double-minded
[ ]	[ ]	[ ]	[ ]	[ ]	Not Spiritually Indifferent
[ ]	[ ]	[ ]	[ ]	[ ]	Not Self-righteous
[ ]	[ ]	[ ]	[ ]	[ ]	No Hardness of Heart
[ ]	[ ]	[ ]	[ ]	[ ]	Aggressively Resists Satan
[ ]	[ ]	[ ]	[ ]	[ ]	Avoids All Idolatry
[ ]	[ ]	[ ]	[ ]	[ ]	Patient and Forbearing
[ ]	[ ]	[ ]	[ ]	[ ]	Fulfill Covenant Requirements
[ ]	[ ]	[ ]	[ ]	[ ]	Avoid Vain Repetition
[ ]	[ ]	[ ]	[ ]	[ ]	Recognize God's Sovereignty
[ ]	[ ]	[ ]	[ ]	[ ]	Pray in Jesus' Name

Ex. = Excellent; V.G. = Very Good; N.I. = Needs Improvement

Plan of Correction:
What are you willing to commit to do, in order to fulfill the covenant requirements of God's Precious Promises -- each of which is a promissory note?

_____

_____

Chapter Seven ~ Pursuing Personal Purity

Ministry Preparedness:

The apostle Peter warned those about to embark in ministry, to: *"Be self-controlled and alert. Your enemy the devil prowls around like a roaring lion looking for someone to devour. Resist him, standing firm in the faith, because you know that your brothers throughout the world are undergoing the same kind of sufferings"* (1 Peter 5:8-9).

The apostle Paul, reflecting on God's precious promises, wrote: *"Since we have these promises, dear friends, **let us purify ourselves from everything that contaminates body and spirit, perfecting holiness out of reverence for God**"* (2 Cor 7:1).

Speaking of his personal experience when commissioning his disciples, Paul said: *"We **put no stumbling block in anyone's path, so that our ministry will not be discredited**. Rather, as servants of God we commend ourselves in every way: in great endurance; in troubles, hardships and distresses; in beatings, imprisonments and riots; in hard work, sleepless nights and hunger; **in purity, understanding, patience and kindness; in the Holy Spirit and in sincere love; in truthful speech and in the power of God;** with weapons of righteousness in the right hand and in the left; through glory and dishonor, bad report and good report; genuine, yet regarded as impostors; known, yet regarded as unknown; dying, and yet we live on; beaten, and yet not killed; sorrowful, yet always rejoicing; poor, yet making many rich; having nothing, and yet possessing everything"* (2 Cor 6:3-10).

The author of the Book of Hebrews, stresses the importance of purity and holiness, saying: *"Make every effort to live in peace with all men and to be holy; **without holiness no one will see the Lord.** See to it that no one misses the grace of God and that no bitter root grows up to cause trouble and defile many"* (Heb 12:14-16).

As these authors indicate, personal purity and holiness is imperative both in resisting the powers of darkness and in witnessing and ministering to others. Without holiness, no one will see the Lord, and without holiness it is impossible to prevent our becoming discredited, thereby becoming a stumbling block in the spiritual path of those we would lead to the Lord. As Spiritual Warriors, purity and holiness must be a central focus in life. One of the more difficult aspects of insuring that our personal purity and holiness meets God's plan for us lies in the problem that we are often unaware of the impurity lodged in our heart.

Destroying Denial:
One of the more difficult aspects of insuring that our personal purity and holiness meets God's plan for us lies in our denial – in the problem that we are often unaware of the impurity lodged in our heart – denying it access into our conscious mind. As King David wrote: *"The heart and mind of man are cunning"* (Ps 64:6); and the prophet Jeremiah confirmed this, saying: *"The heart is deceitful above all things, and desperately wicked: who can know it?"* (Jer 17:9). King David understood this dilemma and cried: *"Search me, O God, and know my heart; test me and know my anxious thoughts. See if there is any offensive way in me, and lead me in the way everlasting"* (Ps 139:23-24).

God's Purification Process:
After describing how deceitfully wicked man's heart is, the prophet Jeremiah provides the solution: *"I the Lord search the heart, I try the reins, even to give every man according to his ways, and according to the fruit of his doings"* (Jer 17:10). ... *"See, I will refine and test them, for what else can I do because of the sin of my people?"* (Jer 9:7b).

Notice that Jeremiah, speaking on behalf of the Lord, says He will both test and refine His people – employing two distinctly different processes to first determine, then enhance, their purity. The prophets Zechariah and Malachai both reference these processes. *"I will refine them like silver and test them like gold"* (Zech 13:9); and, *"He will sit as a refiner and purifier of silver; He will purify the Levites and refine them like gold and silver. Then the Lord will have men who will bring offerings in righteousness"* (Mal 3:3-4).

The Process of Refining
The process of refining, and its application to God's people is referenced throughout Scripture. God tells us that He took us out of a smelting furnace to make us His people. *"But as for you, the Lord took you and brought you out of the iron-smelting furnace, out of Egypt, to be the people of his inheritance, as you now are"* (Dt 4:20). Removed from the iron-smelting furnace (referring to base, or common, metal), the Lord says He will refine us as silver and gold *"The crucible for silver and the furnace for gold, but the Lord tests the heart"* (Pr 17:3).

Silver ore has to go through a refining process called Cupellation in order for the pure silver to be separated from the dross. Cupellation occurs when **the ore is heated to 1,200 degrees** Celsius in a special furnace. First however, the silver ore is placed in a solution containing 30 to 35 percent nitric acid.

It takes one and one-half ounces of nitric acid to dissolve one ounce of silver. The solution produces a white powder called silver chloride. When sodium carbonate is mixed with the silver chloride and placed in a cupellation furnace, the heat causes a chemical reaction that reduces the powder to table salt and silver. The process works without the addition of sodium carbonate as well but then the heat releases poisonous chlorine gas as it produces the pure silver.

Similarly, gold ore is ground to a fine powder, mixed with a chemical solvent -- most commonly cyanide -- which produces a leaching action that separates the gold-bearing carbon. This carbon is then subjected to a hot caustic solution -- usually nitric acid -- which separates the non-ferrous metals from the carbon. Finally, this undifferentiated mass of nonferrous metals is put into a smelting furnace and heated**, in stages, to about 2,100 degrees Fahrenheit or 1150 degrees Celsius**, at which time the refiners add a chemical referred to as flux to separate the gold from the other metals. Both of these processes involve intense heat and fire, suggestive of the cleansing and purifying process God employs within those He loves. This process is first mentioned in Scripture by the prophet Isaiah, who wrote: ***"He will cleanse the bloodstains from Jerusalem by a spirit of judgment and a spirit of fire"*** (Is 4:4-5).

John the Baptist referenced this process, saying: *"I baptize you with water for repentance. But after me will come one who is more powerful than I, whose sandals I am not fit to carry.* ***He will baptize you with the Holy Spirit and with fire.*** *His winnowing fork is in his hand, and he will clear his threshing floor, gathering his wheat into the barn and burning up the chaff with unquenchable fire"* (Mt 3:11-12).

Not only has the Lord told us in advance that He will baptize us with the Holy Spirit and with fire, He tells us the nature of the fire that we will be subjected to: *"See,* ***I have refined you, though not as silver; I have tested you in the furnace of affliction***. *For my own sake, for my own sake, I do this. How can I let myself be defamed? I will not yield my glory to another"* (Is 48:10-11).

The Test:
God in His mercy has not only devised a plan to refine our hearts, but has provided to test us that we may comprehend how pure or impure our heart is. We read about this test in the Book of Amos. The prophet Amos says: *"This is what he showed me: The Lord was standing by a wall that had been built true to plumb, with a plumb line in his hand. And the Lord asked me, "What do you see, Amos?"*

*"A plumb line," I replied. Then **the Lord said, "Look, I am setting a plumb line among my people Israel;** I will spare them no longer"* (Amos 7:7-8). The prophet Isaiah also references the use of the plumb line, saying: *"See, **I lay a stone in Zion, a tested stone, a precious cornerstone for a sure foundation**; the one who trusts will never be dismayed. **I will make justice the measuring line and righteousness the plumb line"** (Is 28:16-17).

Christ the Foundation and Cornerstone
*"**For no one can lay any foundation other than the one already laid, which is Jesus Christ**. If any man builds on this foundation using gold, silver, costly stones, wood, hay or straw, his work will be shown for what it is, because the Day will bring it to light. It will be revealed with fire, and the fire will test the quality of each man's work. If what he has built survives, he will receive his reward. If it is burned up, he will suffer loss; he himself will be saved, but only as one escaping through the flames"* (1 Cor 3:11-15).

"Consequently, you are no longer foreigners and aliens, but fellow citizens with God's people and members of God's household, built on the foundation of the apostles and prophets, with Christ Jesus himself as the chief cornerstone. In him the whole building is joined together and rises to become a holy temple in the Lord. And in him you too are being built together to become a dwelling in which God lives by his Spirit" (Eph 2:19-22).

Christ is the standard for living -- there is no other; and based on this cornerstone, God puts a plumb line alongside our heart to test our righteousness and purity. How can God test a man with a plumb line? The books of First Samuel and First Chronicles define just what it is that God is testing with this plumb and measuring line. Giving Samuel direction and guidance in the selection of a king for Israel, God said to Samuel:

"Do not consider his appearance or his height ... The Lord does not look at the things man looks at. Man looks at the outward appearance, but God looks at the heart." (1 Samuel 16:7). And, King David reminded his son Solomon that *"...the Lord searches [examines] every heart and understands every motive behind the thoughts."* (1 Chronicles 28:9).

The Walls of Your Heart:
Envision, for a moment that you, like Amos of old, could behold God (The Divine One, Creator of the universe) standing alongside you with his plumb line, ready to test your heart (personality).

What would God find? How plumb, how true is your wall -- the wall of your personality? Now imagine that God were to move His plumb line inside your wall (personality) and alongside your "heart," the very core of your being (your axis, if you please). Will your inner-being, your values, your foundational beliefs and life-commandments pass this test? Do your beliefs life-commandments align well with God's universal and immutable values and standards?

Are your values consistent with God's? Do your principles agree with His? Do your ethics meet this integrity test? Are His characteristics and traits those manifest in your life? Are the words that come out of your mouth acceptable to Him? Is your behavior acceptable to Him? Are the intellectual thoughts you entertain acceptable to Him? Are your imaginations pure and acceptable to Him?

God's Blueprint and Design:

God has a plan, or blueprint, for each of our lives. For example, He designed Jeremiah to be a prophet and set him apart, appointing him to this calling prior to his birth. *"Before I formed you in the womb I knew you, before you were born I set you apart; I appointed you as a prophet to the nations"* (Jer 1:5).

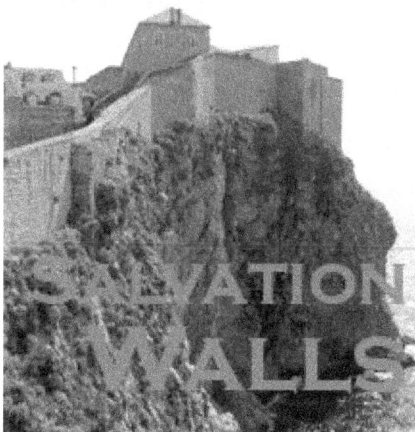

Walls are designed for our protection – protection from the elements, and from intruders. God's walls – those He designed for our hearts -- are no different. Their design is to provide protection and salvation. The prophet Isaiah wrote: *"So this is what the Sovereign Lord says: "See, I lay a stone in Zion, a tested stone, a precious cornerstone for a sure foundation; the one who trusts (therein) will never be dismayed"* (Is 28:16).

"The sacrifices of God are a broken spirit; a broken and contrite heart, O God, you will not despise. In your good pleasure make Zion prosper; build up the walls of Jerusalem" (Ps 51:17-18).

"I will build you with stones of turquoise, your foundations with sapphires. I will make your battlements of rubies, your gates of sparkling jewels, and all your walls of precious stones. All your sons will be taught by the Lord, and great will be your children's peace" (Isa 54:11-13).

Our personality: the walls of our heart – those that we construct on our own – are not those that God designed for us. In fact, they are so alien to God's design and purpose they must be removed before the walls of salvation can be constructed. God is committed to demolish our flimsy walls. We read about this in the Book of Ezekiel.

*"This is what the Sovereign Lord says: Because of your false words and lying visions, I am against you, declares the Sovereign Lord. My hand will be against the prophets who see false visions and utter lying divinations. ... Because they lead my people astray, saying, "Peace," when there is no peace, and because, **when a flimsy wall is built, they cover it with whitewash**, therefore tell those who cover it with whitewash that **it is going to fall**.*

*"Rain will come in torrents, and **I will send hailstones hurtling down, and violent winds will burst forth**. When the wall collapses, will people not ask you, "Where is the whitewash you covered it with?" Therefore this is what the Sovereign Lord says: **In my wrath I will unleash a violent wind, and in my anger hailstones and torrents of rain will fall with destructive fury. I will tear down the wall you have covered with whitewash and will level it to the ground so that its foundation will be laid bare**"* (Ezek 13:8-14).

Man's Gyroscopic Auto-correct System:
Mankind (God's children) were created by his hand, according to His standards. Unfortunately, man's personality -- and even his character -- have been deformed. Sometimes this deformation occurred so early in life that the disfigured result has been accepted as "normal." Yet, beneath this deformation there still exists the original pattern which can be transiently deformed but never permanently altered. Like a gyroscope (pictured right) is continually seeks to correct us and conform us to the original pattern, redirecting us back to the true pathway.

Just as a plumb line temporarily pushed out of line seeks its own when the force is removed, and the gyroscope seeks to keep us stable, so does the human spirit (our true-self or inner-being) seek to govern our life. Spiritual laws, like physical laws, are absolute. They may be temporarily denied but they can never be permanently altered by man. It is these laws at work and this natural tendency of our inner-being to seek its "natural" (spiritual) state (that harmonious connectedness with The Divine) that provides hope.

It is these God ordained, 'natural laws' at work within us that generate the deep emotions of rejection, guilt and shame when the human spirit is out-of-line with the immutable universal standards.

Separated from the one and only, genuine source of truth, man's inner axis – his axiology – becomes bent, resulting in him wobbling, as it were, aimlessly through life. Having desensitized his inner gyroscope designed to keep him from harm and danger, he does not sense those deep motivational emotions. Separated from God, the source of life, love and nurture, man experiences rejection and abandonment, but sees no solution – no way out of his seemingly hopeless situation.

When man attempts to satiate his love-deficit and fill his inner void with mood-altering pleasures, experiences and/or substances, man anaesthetizes the God-given emotions of guilt and shame.

These deep emotions – rejection/ abandonment and guilt/shame – are in reality powerful inner gyroscopes, or servo-mechanisms within our inner guidance system, designed to pull us back on track, to keep us level, and help us find that inner serenity as we once again align ourselves with God's unalterable universal standards. An appropriate response of moving toward The Divine when we experience these emotions would quickly restore our tranquillity.

Unfortunately, few of us have ever seen this concept modeled so when we feel rejected or sense guilt or shame, we reactively move away from authority, away from established principles and standards. We blame The Divine -- and often all authority over our life for the chaos we are experiencing. The result is an increased sense of rejection, greater mood-swings, deeper compulsivities and addictions, and more intense guilt and shame.

Only as one yields to the pull of these inner servo-mechanisms and gyroscopes – motivational emotions such as guilt, healthy shame, repentance, forgiveness, etc., and move toward authority – toward God, His standards, ideals, and particularly His design for our life; only as we embrace His sovereign plan and fulfill His preordained purpose for our life, will we find rest and discover that inner peace that has eluded us.

The words of the old hymn, reproduced on the following page, depict this desperate search for peace, that most have experienced, and directs us to the only solution – to lay our all on the altar of sacrifice, and fulfill God's will for our life.

You have longed for sweet peace, and for faith to increase,

And have earnestly, fervently prayed;

But you cannot have rest, or be perfectly blest,

Until all on the altar is laid.

Is your all on the altar of sacrifice laid?

Your heart, does the Spirit control?

You can only be blest and have peace and sweet rest,

As you yield Him your body and soul.

Would you walk with the Lord in the light of His Word,

And have peace and contentment alway;

You must do His sweet will to be free from all ill;

On the altar your all you must lay.

Oh, we never can know what the Lord will bestow

Of the blessings for which we have prayed,

Till our body and soul He doth fully control,

And our all on the altar is laid.

Who can tell all the love He will send from above!

Oh, how happy our heart will be made!

Oh, what fellowship sweet we shall share at His feet,

When our all on the altar is laid!

Chapter Eight ~ Invoking Spiritual Artillery

After being trained in putting on our spiritual armor and taking up our spiritual weapons, there is another area of major consideration, the support artillery. In contrast to our personal weaponry, artillery of warfare includes those heavy weapons that can accomplish tasks unthinkable for even the best equipped infantryman. Artillery, sometimes referred to as ordnance, includes those weapons too large for one to handle but transportable. This includes: ships, planes, tanks, armored vehicles, torpedoes, missiles, missile and torpedo launchers, etc. To the infantryman facing the enemy, this heavy artillery seems like a God sent gift.

The spiritual warrior has at his/her disposal similar artillery. The apostle Paul refers to them as spiritual gifts. *"Now about spiritual gifts, brothers, I do not want you to be ignorant. You know that when you were pagans, somehow or other you were influenced and led astray to mute idols. Therefore I tell you that no one who is speaking by the Spirit of God says, "Jesus be cursed," and no one can say, "Jesus is Lord," except by the Holy Spirit.* **There are different kinds of gifts, but the same Spirit. There are different kinds of service, but the same Lord. There are different kinds of working, but the same God works all of them in all men**.

"Now to each one the manifestation of the Spirit is given for the common good. To one there is given through the Spirit the **message of wisdom***, to another the* **message of knowledge** *by means of the same Spirit,* **to another faith** *by the same Spirit,* **to another gifts of healing** *by that one Spirit,* **to another miraculous powers***,* **to another prophecy***,* **to another distinguishing (discerning) between spirits***,* **to another speaking in different kinds of tongues, and to still another the interpretation of tongues** *[and* **the gifts of helps and administration** *(vs. 28)]. All these are the work of one and the same Spirit, and he gives them to each one, just as he determines. The body is a unit, though it is made up of many parts; and though all its parts are many, they form one body. ... If one part suffers, every part suffers with it; if one part is honored, every part rejoices with it"* (1 Cor 12:1-12 & 26-28).

Controlling Spiritual Artillery:
In keeping with our metaphor of physical warfare, the spiritual warrior must keep in mind that this artillery is under the control of, and is deployed at the direction of, Holy Spirit, not the warrior. **They are not skills that can be developed, but are gifts -- gifts supplied by Holy Spirit as necessary and appropriate to the occasion.** Like pieces of heavy military artillery, **they may be operated by an individual, but they are not under his/her command.** They are given for the good of all, to provide covering and protection for all, and accomplish those tasks that individual warriors fighting alone cannot.

Practical Illustrations:
To illustrate the intimate interaction between a spiritual warrior and Holy Spirit, and the function of this artillery, let us share some personal experiences.

- **The gift of wisdom:** A message, concept, or bit of wisdom that God reveals supernaturally to the recipient. It may or may not be shared with others. It includes the ability to make godly decisions and give guidance to others that is according to God's will.

  As pastoral counselors, we are often asked for guidance and counsel and it is our practice to take the counselee's request to God, seeking **supernatural wisdom** rather than relying on our own. As we wait on God, Holy Spirit will impress a certain Scripture, or Scriptures, on our heart. Some of the pertinent Scriptures concerning the gift of wisdom include the following:

  - *"Give me **wisdom** and knowledge, that I may lead this people, for who is able to govern this great people of yours?"* (2 Ch 1:10).

  - *"The fear of the Lord is the beginning of **wisdom**; all who follow His precepts have good understanding"* (Ps 111:10).

  - *"**Wisdom** is supreme; therefore get **wisdom**. Though it cost all you have, get understanding. Esteem her, and she will exalt you; embrace her, and she will honor you. She will set a garland of grace on your head and present you with a crown of splendor"* (Pr 4:7-9).

  - *"In him we have redemption through his blood, the forgiveness of sins, in accordance with the riches of God's grace that he lavished on us with all **wisdom** and understanding"* (Eph 1:7-8).

not stopped praying for you and asking God to fill you with the knowledge of his will through all spiritual **wisdom** *and understanding"* (Col 1:9).

- **The gift of knowledge:** A message, concept, or bit of knowledge that God reveals supernaturally to the recipient. It may or may not be shared with others. It gives one an in-depth understanding of a spiritual issue or situation.

On one occasion several years ago while we were working with the 700 Club Mercy Ministries, a young man came in to the ministry looking for clothing. I (Doc) spent an hour or more helping him select some clothing; simultaneously trying to share Christ Jesus. He rebuffed my every endeavor, telling me that he was a Sea Captain and the God he knew was the one he saw in the waves, the birds, etc. As we talked, he drew a small portfolio booklet from his pocket and showed me photos of pictures he had painted.

After he had made his clothing selections, we went into the office where Paula sat with the ministry director. Paula had just returned from the dentist's office and was not speaking too legibly. As I introduced the young man to her and the director, I handed Paula the portfolio. She looked through the snapshots, looked up and in a clear voice said, "I can see from these pictures that you are very close to God." Then, seemingly out of nowhere, Paula said, "And, by the way, it was not God who killed your father, but alcoholism."

At this, the young man fell to the floor sobbing. After recovering a bit, he related -- through intermittent sobs -- that his father had indeed died of alcoholism when he was only seven. Where all of my efforts and appeals had failed, the **word of knowledge** given through Paula, brought immediate conviction. He easily embraced a God that could 'read his mail' and was open to guidance in the way of the Lord.

Some Scriptures pertaining to the gift of **knowledge** include the following: *"The fear of the Lord is the beginning of wisdom, and* **knowledge** *of the Holy One is understanding"* (Pr 9:10).

"To the man who pleases him, God gives wisdom, **knowledge** *and happiness"* (Eccl 2:26). … *"For this reason, since the day we heard about you, we have not stopped praying for you and asking God to fill you with the* **knowledge** *of his will through all spiritual wisdom and understanding"* (Col 1:9-10).

129

*"Grace and peace be yours in abundance through the **knowledge** of God and of Jesus our Lord"* (2 Pe 1:2).

- **The gift of faith:** Knowing that what you hope for, God will provide, having an in-depth conviction about things you cannot see, yet trusting God, believing God's Word, and obeying God, confident that He will fulfill your need or meet your heart's desire. (See Heb 11). The gift of faith enables one to trust God to this depth and encourage others to trust in God's provision, no matter the circumstances.

As we write this, I (Doc) am reminded of one occasion where our rent was overdue and we had no money. On Friday afternoon, our landlord came to our ministry and gave us a three day notice, to either pay our rent or move. We tried to explain our situation -- that we had funds coming within a few days -- but he was unmoved. Saturday's mail came and no funds. Sunday morning, we went to Sunday school and church, praying and believing that God heard our prayers and would meet our need.

That afternoon, as Paula and I lay on our bed reading our Bible and praying, the phone rang. Picking up the phone, one of our counselees said that he really needed to see us and asked if we were going to be home for a few minutes. Confirming that we would be there, we sat, wondering what crisis he was facing. He arrived shortly and handed us an envelope, telling us that God had told him to come give this to us. As quickly as he had come, he was gone, and looking inside the envelope, was $550.00 -- the exact amount needed to pay our rent! Some Scriptures concerning the gift of faith that you may want to commit to memory include the following: *"Whatever you ask for in prayer, believe that you have received it, and it will be yours"* (Mk 11:24).

- *"The righteous will live by faith"* (Rom 1:17).
- *"We live by faith, not by sight"* (2 Cor 5:7-8).
- *"Those who have faith are blessed along with Abraham, the man of faith"* (Gal 3:9).
- *"We do not want you to become lazy, but to imitate those who through faith and patience inherit what has been promised"* (Heb 6:12).
- *"Let us fix our eyes on Jesus, the author and perfecter of our faith"* (Heb 12:2).
- *"This is the victory that has overcome the world, even our faith"* (1 Jn 5:4-5).

- **The gift of healing:** The supernatural ability to release healing to a person in their body or soul. It is the miraculous ability to use God's healing power to restore a person who is sick, injured, or suffering emotionally.

There are many instances we could recount from our twenty plus years of ministry but, one of the more outstanding ones involved the healing of a woman we never even met! Working the telephones for a television prayer ministry, we received a call one morning from an elderly woman who asked for prayer for healing. She explained that she had diabetes and recently had one of her legs amputated. Now her other leg was beginning to turn black and she was in fear -- fear that she would lose that leg too and be unable to care for herself or her husband.

Although she felt fear, she recounted that as she watched the television program that morning, she felt faith rising up in her -- faith that if she availed herself of prayer, she would be healed. As we prayed, she suddenly cried out, "it's turning pink: my leg is turning pink!"

We never met that woman but several years later, we became acquainted with her neighbor who testified that this woman who had called seeking healing had recently died; but that from the moment we prayed, she testified, the diabetes she was afflicted with went into remission. She outlived her husband, and died from natural causes at a good old age. A few of the many Scriptures dealing with the gift of healing, which you may wish to commit to memory, include the following:

- *"For you who revere my name, the sun of righteousness will rise with healing in its wings"* (Mal 4:2).

- *"He called his twelve disciples to him and gave them authority to drive out evil spirits and to heal every disease and sickness"* (Mt 10:1).

- *"So they set out and went from village to village, preaching the gospel and healing people everywhere"* (Lk 9:6).

- *"Heal the sick, raise the dead, cleanse those who have leprosy, drive out demons. Freely you have received, freely give"* (Mt 10:8).

- *"He sent them out to preach the kingdom of God and to heal the sick"* (Lk 9:2-3).

131

- *"Heal the sick who are there and tell them, 'The kingdom of God is near you'"* (Lk 10:9-10).

- *"Lord, consider their (the enemies) threats and enable your servants to speak your word with great boldness. Stretch out your hand to heal and perform miraculous signs and wonders through the name of your holy servant, Jesus"* (Acts 4:29-30).

- **The gift of miracles:** The ability to perform supernatural acts by the Spirit of God. This gift enables one to perform signs and wonders that give authenticity to God's Word and the Gospel message. I (Doc) cannot recall a clear case of Holy Spirit using either of us in this manner. However, I have personal knowledge of a number of instances that a friend or acquaintance was used in this way. One instance that comes to mind had to do with a friend in the mission field who was trying to explain Christ's crucifixion -- that he had been nailed to the cross.

The aborigines he was ministering among had never seen a nail and simply could not comprehend what he was talking about. Returning home that evening a bit frustrated and discouraged, he and his wife prayed earnestly that God would sovereignty intervene.

The next morning, they arose, and as his wife was fixing breakfast, my friend opened a case of tomato juice that had arrived from the mainland USA. Removing one of the large, 40 oz. cans from the box, he shook it as he reached for the can opener. Then, he stopped and shook it again -- believing he heard something rattling around inside. Opening the can, he discovered an old, rusty, 8" spike!

Thanking God, my friend gulped down his breakfast then hurried to the village to exhibit the nail. In no time at all, the man who had challenged him the previous afternoon, together with his wife, family, neighbors and friends, all embraced our Lord and Savior, Jesus Christ -- all because of a single old rusty nail.

A few of the Scriptures dealing with the manifestation of signs and wonders, that those who receive this gift may wish to commit to memory, include the following:

- *He performs wonders that cannot be fathomed, miracles that cannot be counted"* (Job 9:10).

- *"You are the God who performs miracles; you display your power among the peoples"* (Ps 77:14).

- *"When they believed Philip as he preached the good news of the kingdom of God and the name of Jesus Christ, they were baptized, both men and women. Simon (the sorcerer) himself believed and was baptized. And he followed Philip everywhere, astonished by the great signs and miracles he saw"* (Acts 8:12-13).

- *"God did extraordinary miracles through Paul, so that even handkerchiefs and aprons that had touched him were taken to the sick, and their illnesses were cured and the evil spirits left them"* (Acts 19:11-12).

- *"This salvation, which was first announced by the Lord, was confirmed to us by those who heard him. God also testified to it by signs, wonders and various miracles, and gifts of the Holy Spirit distributed according to his will"* (Heb 2:3-4).

- *"They devoted themselves to the apostles' teaching and to the fellowship, to the breaking of bread and to prayer. Everyone was filled with awe, and many wonders and miraculous signs were done by the apostles"* (Acts 2:42-44).

- *"The apostles performed many miraculous signs and wonders among the people"* (Acts 5:12).

- *"Now Stephen, a man full of God's grace and power, did great wonders and miraculous signs among the people"* (Acts 6:8-9).

- *"Paul and Barnabas spent considerable time there (in Iconium), speaking boldly for the Lord, who confirmed the message of his grace by enabling them to do miraculous signs and wonders"* (Acts 14:3).

- *"The things that mark an apostle [are] signs, wonders and miracles"* (2 Cor 12:12).

- **The gift of prophecy:** The supernatural ability to receive a message from God, and proclaim that message, to edify, exhort and comfort the body of Christ or a believer. To speak as moved by the Holy Spirit. Not all prophecies contain predictions about the future.

The Lord has, over the past two years, used the two of us (Doc and Paula) as a prophetic team. We try to honor a morning time to meet with the Lord, usually spending between an hour and one-half and two hours interceding for our families, our students, our counselees and whomsoever else God puts on our hearts. As we intercede for an individual or ministry, God usually gives me (Doc) one or more Scriptures. As we look them up and read them, Paula summarizes them in writing, while we both pray for understanding.

Often, Holy Spirit illuminates our hearts, clarifying how the Scriptures apply to the particular person or ministry we are interceding for. When this happens, and as directed, we share the information with the person or ministry director. Frequently, however, God merely gives us the Scriptures, counting on us to share these with the person or responsible party, having faith that Holy Spirit will illuminate that person's heart, giving them the interpretative application of the text or texts.

- **The gift of discerning spirits**: The supernatural ability to know what is from God and what is not -- to determine whether or not a message, person, or event is truly from God. It includes receiving Divine instruction to reveal a demonic spirit or influence and bring God's power (Jesus' blood) and God's love (Jesus' crucifixion and resurrection) in its place.

To effectively employ the power of prayer, one needs to receive, and exercise, the gift of discernment. Demonstrating the dynamic outcome when prayer is combined with discernment, God's Word says:

- *"They are a nation without sense, there is no discernment in them. If only they were wise and would understand this and discern what their end will be! How could one man chase a thousand, or two put ten thousand to flight!"* (Dt 32:28-30).

Practical Application:
Faced with a problem in ministry recently, we sought discernment, praying: *"Dear Lord, Messiah, Father and Holy Spirit, thank you for our time together. Regarding Mr. 'x', is he a deceiver -- a seducer of spirits -- as mentioned in 2 Pet and Jude? He wants to help us in ministry, however, I have misgivings concerning his intentions. Show us Your Word, Lord; give us wisdom, understanding and discernment, please. You've given us so much personally, so much for the church to guide its growth. Thank you for guiding and protecting."*

God's answer was to direct our thoughts to Ezekiel, chapters 37 and 17. *"The hand of the Lord was upon me, and he brought me out by the Spirit of the Lord and set me in the middle of a valley; it was full* of bones. He led me back and forth among them, and I saw a great many bones on the floor of the valley, bones that were very dry. He asked me, "Son of man, can these bones live?" I said, "O Sovereign Lord, you alone know."

"Then he said to me, "Prophesy to these bones and say to them, 'Dry bones, hear the word of the Lord! This is what the Sovereign Lord says to these bones: I will make breath enter you, and you will come to life. I will attach tendons to you and make flesh come upon you and cover you with skin; I will put breath in you, and you will come to life. Then you will know that I am the Lord.'"

"So I prophesied as I was commanded. And as I was prophesying, there was a noise, a rattling sound, and the bones came together, bone to bone. I looked, and tendons and flesh appeared on them and skin covered them, but there was no breath in them. Then he said to me, "Prophesy to the breath; prophesy, son of man, and say to it, 'This is what the Sovereign Lord says: Come from the four winds, O breath, and breathe into these slain, that they may live.'" So I prophesied as he commanded me, and breath entered them; they came to life and stood up on their feet – a vast army.

"Then he said to me: "Son of man, these bones are the whole house of Israel. They say, 'Our bones are dried up and our hope is gone; we are cut off.' Therefore prophesy and say to them: 'This is what the Sovereign Lord says: O my people, I am going to open your graves and bring you up from them; I will bring you back to the land of Israel. Then you, my people, will know that I am the Lord, when I open your graves and bring you up from them. I will put my Spirit in you and you will live, and I will settle you in your own land. Then you will know that I the Lord have spoken, and I have done it, declares the Lord.'"

The word of the Lord came to me: "Son of man, take a stick of wood and write on it, 'Belonging to Judah and the Israelites associated with him.' Then take another stick of wood, and write on it, 'Ephraim's stick, belonging to Joseph and all the house of Israel associated with him.' Join them together into one stick so that they will become one in your hand.

"When your countrymen ask you, 'Won't you tell us what you mean by this?' say to them, 'This is what the Sovereign Lord says: I am going to take the stick of Joseph — which is in Ephraim's hand — and of the Israelite tribes associated with him, and join it to Judah's stick, making them a single stick of wood, and they will become one in my hand.'

"When your countrymen ask you, 'Won't you tell us what you mean by this?' say to them, 'This is what the Sovereign Lord says: I am going to take the stick of Joseph — which is in Ephraim's hand — and of the Israelite tribes associated with him, and join it to Judah's stick, making them a single stick of wood, and they will become one in my hand. Hold before their eyes the sticks you have written on and say to them, 'This is what the Sovereign Lord says: I will take the Israelites out of the nations where they have gone. I will gather them from all around and bring them back into their own land. I will make them one nation in the land, on the mountains of Israel. There will be one king over all of them and they will never again be two nations or be divided into two kingdoms. They will no longer defile themselves with their idols and vile images or with any of their offenses, for I will save them from all their sinful backsliding, and I will cleanse them. They will be my people, and I will be their God.

"'My servant David will be king over them, and they will all have one shepherd. They will follow my laws and be careful to keep my decrees. They will live in the land I gave to my servant Jacob, the land where your fathers lived. They and their children and their children's children will live there forever, and David my servant will be their prince forever. I will make a covenant of peace with them; it will be an everlasting covenant. I will establish them and increase their numbers, and I will put my sanctuary among them forever. My dwelling place will be with them; I will be their God, and they will be my people. Then the nations will know that I the Lord make Israel holy, when my sanctuary is among them forever'" (Eze 37 NIV).

From these words -- "revival: speak to them and they will live" -- we perceived that God was giving a green light for us to include this individual in our ministry efforts. Reading the footnotes out of my New King James Version, several things impressed me, Paula. Verse 3 suggests that there is no limit in what God can, and will, do for us. Another concept that seems clear from verse 4 is that we need to prophesy -- speaking forth the Word of God. Verse 5 says to speak breath (Holy Spirit) into lifeless bodies. Verse 6 indicates the outcome saying: "you shall live" -- promising rebirth from spiritual death, effectuated by divine power. The bones symbolized the whole house of Israel. They were dry, indicating they were spiritually dead. They were despondent and dejected without hope of resurrection as the people of the living God. They were described as being disassembled and disbursed before being rejoined and rebuilt. The major thrust is the coming spiritual rebirth of God's chosen people through the agency of His Spirit.

Applying this to the church today, Spiritual rebirth will miraculously revive and restore God's people to what He had intended them to be in the beginning. The Lord entered into an everlasting covenant with Abraham and the family of faith. God is establishing His church as His sanctuary.

From here, God led us to Ezekiel 17. *"The word of the Lord came to me: "Son of man, set forth an allegory and tell the house of Israel a parable. Say to them, 'This is what the Sovereign Lord says: A great eagle with powerful wings, long feathers and full plumage of varied colors came to Lebanon. Taking hold of the top of a cedar, he broke off its topmost shoot and carried it away to a land of merchants, where he planted it in a city of traders. He took some of the seed of your land and put it in fertile soil. He planted it like a willow by abundant water, and it sprouted and became a low, spreading vine. Its branches turned toward him, but its roots remained under it. So it became a vine and produced branches and put out leafy boughs.*

"But there was another great eagle with powerful wings and full plumage. The vine now sent out its roots toward him from the plot where it was planted and stretched out its branches to him for water. It had been planted in good soil by abundant water so that it would produce branches, bear fruit and become a splendid vine. "Say to them, 'This is what the Sovereign Lord says: Will it thrive? Will it not be uprooted and stripped of its fruit so that it withers? All its new growth will wither. It will not take a strong arm or many people to pull it up by the roots. Even if it is transplanted, will it thrive? Will it not wither completely when the east wind strikes it — wither away in the plot where it grew?'"

"Then the word of the Lord came to me: "Say to this rebellious house, 'Do you not know what these things mean?' Say to them: 'The king of Babylon went to Jerusalem and carried off her king and her nobles, bringing them back with him to Babylon. Then he took a member of the royal family and made a treaty with him, putting him under oath. He also carried away the leading men of the land, so that the kingdom would be brought low, unable to rise again, surviving only by keeping his treaty. But the king rebelled against him by sending his envoys to Egypt to get horses and a large army. Will he succeed? Will he who does such things escape? Will he break the treaty and yet escape?

"As surely as I live, declares the Sovereign Lord, he shall die in Babylon, in the land of the king who put him on the throne, whose oath he despised and whose treaty he broke. Pharaoh with his

mighty army and great horde will be of no help to him in war, when ramps are built and siege works erected to destroy many lives. He despised the oath by breaking the covenant. Because he had given his hand in pledge and yet did all these things, he shall not escape.

"Therefore this is what the Sovereign Lord says: As surely as I live, I will bring down on his head my oath that he despised and my covenant that he broke. I will spread my net for him, and he will be caught in my snare. I will bring him to Babylon and execute judgment upon him there because he was unfaithful to me. All his fleeing troops will fall by the sword, and the survivors will be scattered to the winds. Then you will know that I the Lord have spoken.

This is what the Sovereign Lord says: I myself will take a shoot from the very top of a cedar and plant it; I will break off a tender sprig from its topmost shoots and plant it on a high and lofty mountain. On the mountain heights of Israel I will plant it; it will produce branches and bear fruit and become a splendid cedar. Birds of every kind will nest in it; they will find shelter in the shade of its branches. All the trees of the field will know that I the Lord bring down the tall tree and make the low tree grow tall. I dry up the green tree and make the dry tree flourish. I the Lord have spoken, and I will do it" (Eze 17 NIV).

Chapter 17, verses 3 to 10, introduce a metaphorical riddle -- a contest between two kings. **The allegory's main thrust is to guide the reader.** In verses 11 to 21, the first great eagle represents the king of Babylon -- who overthrew the highest branch of the tree representing the king of Jerusalem and Judah, taking God's people into captivity. He left but a few of the Israelites in the land, represented by the low spreading vine. The other great eagle represents the King of Egypt, who enticed most of those remaining in the land to defect and come to Egypt. Thus, Israel failed to prosper, but was slain and scattered.

The people of Israel accused God of being unfair, however, Ezekiel, referencing Jeremiah's prophecies, pointed out that their sins --past and present -- make God's action fair and just. Here, the Lord explains His grounds for using Babylon (representing the powers of darkness) to judge Judah (representative of His people). On the basis of our covenant relationship with God, when we enter into a covenant relationship with the powers of darkness [which is idolatry and spiritual adultery], we give God just cause to bring judgment against us.

By entering into a treaty with Egypt, many of the remnant of the

Israelites were slain and growth was stifled. Zedikiah, the leader of this mutiny, was himself defeated and killed (vs 15-16; Is 30:1-5). Referring back to the metaphor, God Himself, chose the 'tender ones' to rule His people, who were the ancestors of Jesus Christ. Each of Christ's ancestors prophesied concerning his coming. The establishment of the cedar twig over Israel will make the nation a fruitful and majestic cedar.

From this, I discerned that while we are presently in a spiritual battle, our enemies will be brought down and God's church will flourish and prevail against the gates of hell, until He returns to rule. Combining these Scriptures with the footnotes that provided some clarity, and discernment by Holy Spirit, I have faith that we will experience revival and that the church leaders will be ready for this move of the Spirit.

We have a part to play in this – that of spiritual warfare – incorporating prayer and discernment to receive His direction before we take action.

Ask God for direction. *"If any of you lacks wisdom, he should ask God, who gives generously to all without finding fault, and it will be given to him. But when he asks, he must believe and not doubt, because he who doubts is like a wave of the sea, blown and tossed by the wind"* (Jas 1:5-7).

God had answered our prayer in detail. Desiring confirmation in applying it, we met with our pastor. While meeting with him, in prayer, we received Psalm 46. *"God is our refuge and strength, an ever-present help in trouble. Therefore we are unafraid, even if the earth gives way, even if the mountains tumble into the depths of the sea, even if its waters rage and foam, and mountains shake at its turbulence. (Selah).*

"There is a river whose streams gladden the city of God, the holy habitation of 'Elyon (Zion) — God is in the city. It will not be moved — when daybreak comes, God will help it. Nations were in turmoil, kingdoms were moved; his voice thundered forth, and the earth melted away. Adonai-Tzva'ot (The Lord of Hosts) is with us, our fortress, the God of Ya'akov. (Selah)

"Come and see the works of Adonai, the astounding deeds he has done on the earth. To the ends of the earth he makes wars cease — he breaks the bow, snaps the spear, burns the shields in the fire. "Desist, and learn that I am God, supreme over the nations, supreme over the earth." Adonai-Tzva'ot (the Lord of Hosts) is with us, our fortress, the God of Ya'akov (Jacob)" (CJB).

139

God will lead us into this non-physical, unseen, spiritual battle. He will guide our every word -- our weapons of warfare. And, assures us victory. Revival is coming! The church will be ready: they will respond and be filled with the Spirit! Following is the model God has imparted to us, that we desire to impart/transfer to each of you.

- **The gift of tongues**: It's first use is a supernatural ability to speak another language not known by the believer speaking it. Its second use is a supernatural ability to speak another language not known by the believer speaking it; to build up the body of Christ when the message is interpreted. It is primarily the ability to speak in a foreign language that you do not have knowledge of, in order to communicate with someone who speaks that language. It may on occasion also be the utterance of language of the Holy Spirit, known as glossolalia (speaking in an unknown tongue).

- **The gift of interpreting tongues**: Supernatural ability to translate tongues into a clear message, declaring the message to all that are present to edify, exhort and comfort the body of Christ. It includes the ability to translate the tongues being spoken and communicate the message back to others in your own language.

- **The gift of administration**: God-given insight into when something needs to be done, who can do it, how it can be completed, and how to lead those people to get it accomplished. Includes being able to keep things organized and in accordance with God's principles.

- **The gift of helps:** A heart to care for and encourage those who are not able to care for themselves and whom no one else would care for. Knowing who to help and when to help -- having the desire and ability to help others, to do whatever is necessary to get a task accomplished.

Chapter Nine ~ Practicing for Combat

The Importance of Practice:

We are at war -- spiritual warfare -- engaged in a battle that will determine the eternal destiny of our own soul, our family members, the church, the mission-field of the world, and the conflict in the heavenlies -- against the principalities and powers of darkness. Foreseeing our day, the Old Testament prophet, Joel, wrote:

"Proclaim this among the nations: Prepare for war! Rouse the warriors! Let all the fighting men draw near and attack. Beat your plowshares into swords and your pruning hooks into spears. Let the weakling say, 'I am strong!' Come quickly, all you nations from every side, and assemble there. Bring down your warriors, O Lord! 'Let the nations be roused; let them advance into the Valley of Jehoshaphat, for there I will sit to judge all the nations on every side" (Joel 3:9-12).

As previously explained, the Valley of Jehoshaphat refers to God's judgment, judgment that enters every battlefield, or area, where the powers of darkness have made an advance against God and His family -- the family of man.

The Battlefields:

There are five battlefields, or war theaters, in the spiritual conflict of the cosmos: 1) the soul; 2) the family; 3) the church; 4) the world; 5) the heavenlies.

As one would prepare for any battle, we begin by winning the internal battle -- the battlefield in our soul. Satan's primary effort is to gain the victory over our soul. If successful in this, the other battlefields fall without effort. There is an old proverb that says: *"God formed us, Satan deformed us, man may reform us, but only God can transform us."* Taking this into account, we begin to carry out the admonition of Paul who wrote: *"Be transformed by the renewing of your mind (soul)"* (Rom 12:2).

If you will recall, we pointed out in chapter four, that when we embark on the mission of casting out unclean spirits, we are entering an arena where we will have direct contact with the evil spirits, or demons. Thus, before engaging in this area of ministry, it is essential that our own spirit be cleansed from sin, our mind renewed, and our soul transformed, so that the enemies of our soul have no doorway, or foothold, to bring an accusation against us. This requires purifying our thoughts, destroying our ungodly imaginations and replacing misbeliefs with truth.

This will enable us to exercise the gift of the Spirit, in discerning between clean and unclean spirits.

Christ also stressed the importance of readiness, and the practice necessary to achieve it, relaying the following parable: *"I will show you what he is like who comes to me and **hears my words and puts them into practice**. He is like a man building a house, who dug down deep and laid the foundation on rock. When a flood came, the torrent struck that house but could not shake it, because it was well built. But the one who **hears my words and does not put them into practice** is like a man who built a house on the ground without a foundation. The moment the torrent struck that house, it collapsed and its destruction was complete"* (Luke 6:47-49).

On another occasion, *"Jesus' mother and brothers came to see him, but they were not able to get near him because of the crowd. Someone told him, "Your mother and brothers are standing outside, wanting to see you." He replied, "My mother and brothers are those who hear God's word and put it into practice"* (Luke 8:19-21). Comprehending the importance of practice -- spelling the difference between winning or losing the warfare against the enemy of our souls, the apostle, Paul, wrote: *"Whatever you have learned, or received, or heard from me, or seen in me — put it into practice. And the God of peace will be with you"* (Phil 4:9).

Christ provided his apostles hands-on, intensive discipleship training for three and one-half years, before sending them into the battle. At first, they ministered only to those who knew the truth, but were themselves not practicing it (Lk 9:1-7; 10:1-8). Returning, they expressed their enthusiasm, saying: "Lord, even the demons submit to us in your name" (Luke 10:17).

After training them and providing them opportunity to practice what they had learned and witnessed; just prior to his ascension into heaven, Christ commissioned them to: *"Go into all the world and preach the good news to all creation. Whoever believes and is baptized will be saved, but whoever does not believe will be condemned. And these signs will accompany those who believe: In my name they will drive out demons; they will speak in new tongues; ... they will place their hands on sick people, and they will get well"* (Mark 16:15-18).

As we have demonstrated in chapter 10, "The Seed of Satan", of our book, "Mysteries of the Bible, Vol. 1 - The Primeval Era", J.V. And P.M. Potter, Advocare Publishing, Redding, CA, 2009, all diseases, illnesses and life-controlling problems are at their root, caused by, or associated with demons. Therefore, expelling demons incorporates healing, and visa-versa.

Updating Christ's Commission:
Following Christ's ascension, all of his apostles, except James and Peter; and most of his disciples, launched out on missionary trips. Within the first century, these men and their disciples, carried the Gospel beyond Jerusalem, as far as India, China, Pakistan, Korea and Central America. In contrast, most 21st. Century Christians have never been on a single missionary trip. Many have never even invited a single person to accept their Lord and Savior, Jesus Christ. The primary reason: most have never been taught how. In short, they have not been discipled. Moreover, of those who have been discipled, few have stepped out in faith to practice the soul winning and healing ministry taught them.

Understanding Discipleship:
Recently, I (Doc) asked our Sunday morning church attendees, how many were disciples. Every one of them raised their hands, which sadly, demonstrated how little most Christians know about what it means to be a disciple. The Greek word translated as 'disciple' is 'mathetes', a form of the word, 'matheo', a term used to identify a 'teacher-learner' -- a pupil who is putting what he/she is learning into practice by teaching others. Understanding this, we challenge each of you to examine your heart and answer the question -- are you truly a disciple of our Lord and Savior, Jesus Christ? We challenge you to pray the prayer of David, and follow God's response: *"Search me, O God, and know my heart; test me and know my anxious thoughts. See if there is any offensive way in me, and lead me in the way everlasting"* (Ps 139:23-24).

In Chapter 4, we learned that one of the weapons of spiritual warfare is *casting out demons* -- those living in people, not those operating in the air [the unseen] (Mt 10:1; Mk 6:7,13; 16:17-18; Lk 9:1-2). We focused on the fact that *"The reason the Son of God appeared was to destroy the devil's work"* (1 Jn 3:8); and that Christ has appointed us -- His disciples -- to carry out this task: *"As the Father has sent me, I am sending you"* (Jn 20:20.

Christ explicitly appointed his disciples -- you and I -- to *"heal the sick, raise the dead, cleanse those who have leprosy (diseases), [and] drive out demons"* (Mt 10:8). And, following His example, we should, no doubt, begin by practicing our ministry to the household of faith. His instruction was: *"Do not go among the Gentiles or enter any town of the Samaritans. Go rather to the lost sheep of Israel. As you go, preach this message: 'The kingdom of heaven is near"* (Mt 10:5-8).

Putting Christ's and David's admonition together, the apostle, Paul provides an excellent pattern for commencing this ministry -- practicing our training by praying for one another: **"Openly confess to one another therefore your faults (your cracks or weaknesses, your false steps and your offenses) and pray for one another, so that you may be healed and restored [body, soul and spirit]; for the earnest (heartfelt, continuing) prayer of a righteous man is tremendously powerful in its working"** (James 5:16).

This incorporates another of our weapons of warfare, that our last lesson (chapter 5) focused on -- the ministry of prayer. As indicated, our success in spiritual warfare relies on our practicing a whole panoply, or symphony of prayer. Remember, we have been instructed to *"pray in the spirit on all occasions with all kinds of prayers and requests, being alert and always praying for all the saints"* (Eph 6:18). Praying for the saints -- those of the household of faith -- is the best place to begin practicing spiritual warfare.

We are all subject to demonic attacks since disobedience to God provides a doorway, or foothold, for demons (Eph 4:26), and *"all have sinned and come short of the glory of God"* (Rom 3:23). Christians cannot be demon possessed, since possession infers having given ownership of one's self to the demons; and since Christians have surrendered themselves to Christ, they cannot belong to Christ and the demons. However, Christians can be, and are, both oppressed by, and infested with, demons.

Christians, almost without exception, understand that we can be oppressed by demons, but many question the idea that one can be infested by demons and yet still be a Christian. But, Jesus employed a parable and metaphor, both of which support this concept. Employing a parable, to illustrate the importance of discipleship, Jesus said: *"When an evil spirit comes out of a man, it goes through arid places seeking rest and does not find it. Then it says, 'I will return to the house I left.' When it arrives, it finds the house unoccupied, swept clean and put in order. Then it goes and takes with it seven other spirits more wicked than itself, and they go in and live there. And the final condition of that man is worse than the first"* (Mt 12:43-45).

In this parable, the owner of the house sweeps the house, putting it in order, yet fails to fill it with other things, indicating that the owner had control, or possession, of the house. In another place, Jesus employed a metaphor of a house with many rooms: *"In my Father's house are many rooms"* (John 14:2).

While the 'house' in this Scripture references the Cosmos, since heaven is God's home; we are also the temple, or home, of God. This metaphor and the parable referenced above, suggests that within each of us is, as it were, many rooms, some of which may -- at our invitation -- be occupied by Christ, Father God and Holy Spirit. At the same time, we may not have made Christ Jesus, Lord of our Life, surrendering ownership to the indwelling Holy Spirit.

This being the case, those areas -- rooms if you please -- that have not been surrendered to God, may be occupied, or infested, by demons, since the fact that God, Who is a Spirit, can inhabit us without having full possession of us, witnesses to the fact that we can be inhabited, or infested by demons, without being possessed -- while we still consider ourselves a Christian. Understanding this, the weapon of spiritual cleansing -- the sweeping of the house -- and furnishing it so it is inviting to Holy Spirit -- through discipleship -- becomes the paramount task for those training for full combat spiritual warfare.

Discipleship, as we have indicated, is a process -- one that should not be entered into lightly, nor one that should be rushed through. But, first things first: before furnishing the rooms of our soul in a manner inviting to Holy Spirit; we must first sweep it clean. The apostle, Paul, describes this task as one of renovation: *"Don't be conformed to the god of this age, but be transformed by the renewing (renovation or retrofitting) of your mind (soul), so that you may be able to discern what the good, pleasing and perfect will of God is"* (Rom 12:2). Only through the process of cleansing and renovation can we learn of God's will for our life. The renovation of a structure involves not just superficial cleaning, but the gutting of the structure -- clear down to the frame. Keeping this metaphor of renovating building, there are a number of steps required.

1. **Step one involves taking an inventory of needs**: this step is what David no doubt envisioned when he invited God to search his heart and expose anything offensive therein. It is a preparatory step that the others are based on, so must be undertaken thoroughly. The Bible pretty much condenses man's sins into two categories:
   a. Idolatry: making an idol of any animate or inanimate object and worshipping that idol as though it had some innate power to save, cure or heal.

   b. Adultery: making an idol of any other being -- human or demon – and worshipping that being as a god, as though it had the ability to save, cure, heal or help.

Completing a thorough inventory demands that one write down the names of activities, people, places, things, and incidents in one's life that have involved either type of sin. This includes:

    a. All intimate relationships, sexual or otherwise,

    b. All sexual expressions outside of marriage, including sexual fantasies, pornography, masturbation, telephone sex, etc.,

    c. All hurtful, wounding relationships,

    d. All dependent relationships, those you depended on in lieu of God,

    e. Every false religion, including psychic readings, astrology, numerology, Ouija board, etc.,

    f. Every secret society such as the Masonic Lodge, Knights of Columbus, The Latter-day Saints, or other organization part of, or emanating out of, the Great White Brotherhood,

    g. Involvement in Christian cults,

    h. All life-controlling problems such as addictions, obsessive-compulsive behavior patterns,

    i. All false beliefs and negative life-commandments.

2. **Prayer Ministry:** In the presence of your counseling group, your spiritual growth group, your counselor, or with one or more individuals you maintain spiritual accountability to, begin to put into practice the admonition of James 5:16 -- of confessing your faults to another and praying for one another as you are led by Holy Spirit.

3. **Renounce all those ungodly things identified above.** Praying aloud a prayer such as those following; and if you are married and have children, you will want to break off these sinful patterns not only in your own life, but in your partner -- since they share in them through intimate contact, and in your children, who are subject to them genetically through cross-generational, familial spiritual oppression.

Following your own prayer of confession and renunciation, by having your pastoral counselor, prayer partner, counseling or spiritual growth group, anoint you and pray for you, cutting those things out of your life, commanding the associated demon spirits to depart, and minister healing to your soul and spirit in the Name of our Lord and Savior, Jesus Christ.

Pray aloud the following prayer, which applies to most of those things identified in your inventory: *"My Heavenly Father, I renounce all of my sins of commission and omission -- including all those identified in my inventory. I renounce and turn away from all of these activities (--name them--) and from past relationships, including (--name them--), in the Name of Jesus, and through the power of Indwelling Holy Spirit. I repent, turning my soul and spirit to you. According to Your promise, I receive by faith, Your forgiveness of everything confessed to you, and your cleansing of my conscience, through the blood of Jesus Christ (Heb 9:14-22). I ask you, in Jesus Name, to erase all my sin record according to your promise (Col 2:14 & Is 43:25); removing them from your Book of Remembrance, and from Satan's record, by and through the precious blood of Jesus, my Savior and my Lord; and I ask that you create in me a clean heart and a right spirit in Jesus' Name (Ps 51:10).*

4. **Embrace God's promise**, that *"there is no condemnation for those who are in Christ Jesus, because through Jesus, the law of the Spirit of Life has set me free from the law of sin and death"* (Rom 8:1-2). Let this truth sink into your heart, and repeat: *"Satan no longer has any unsettled claim against me. He has no longer any right to accuse or harass me. Having received the forgiveness of God, I now forgive myself in Jesus Name. I renounce each and every ungodly relationship and every ungodly activity I have ever been engaged in, in Jesus' Name. I invite Holy Spirit to cut from my spirit, all relationship ties to every ungodly relationship and activity, in Jesus' Name. I have nailed them all on the cross of Calvary and am washed in the blood of Jesus, my Savior."*

5. **Specifically break every ungodly spirit-tie** [often erroneously referred to as soul-ties]. Pray aloud the following: *"Since Scripture tells me that sexual intimacy creates both physical and spiritual ties (Mal 2:15; 1 Cor 6:15-16), I thereby release each and every person with whom I have had an ungodly relationship into Your hands, confessing my part, granting forgiveness to the other party, and asking your forgiveness, God, for both of us. I ask you, Heavenly Father, to assign to me, ministering spirits,*

to carry out the necessary soul restoration and care. These things I ask in the Name of my Lord and Savior, Jesus Christ.

6. **Deal with Generational Patterns:** Understanding that some patterns of sin are transmitted from one generation to the next -- even to the third and fourth generations (Ex 20:5; Dt 5:9-10), that certain patterns of sin -- such as sexual sins -- can be transmitted cross-generationally for ten generations (Dt 23:2); and that the goodness of one generation is transmitted cross-generationally, up to a thousand generations (Ex 20:5; Dt 5:10), pray aloud the following prayer:

> *"Father God, I approach your throne of grace in and through the saving power of the blood of my Lord and Savior, Jesus Christ, and through the power of indwelling Holy Spirit, I now hereby renounce and break off every ungodly pattern of sin entering my life from either my mother's or my father's pedigree, back to the tenth generation; and I call forth every pattern of godliness and goodness, from both my mother's and my father's pedigree, back to a thousand generations."*

7. Renounce Misbeliefs: Recognizing that every culture has certain besetting misbeliefs and associated sins, such as the ancient Celtic Druidism, the Welsh mythology, the Irish little people, Animism among Native Americans and Africans, Pantheism among Europeans, etc., pray aloud the following prayer:

> *"Father God, I approach your throne of grace in and through the saving power of the blood of my Lord and Savior, Jesus Christ, and through the power of indwelling Holy Spirit, I now hereby renounce and break off every ungodly cultural false-religion, false-doctrine, occult and religious spirits, legalism, materialism, and spirits of (--name them--) and associated misbeliefs and rituals, and I command every demon spirit of darkness associated with them to depart from me and never return."*

8. **Take Your Position in Christ:** Conclude each prayer ministry session -- for yourself or for others, when you are ministering to them -- with prayers similar to the ones following:

> • *"Seated at the right hand of Jesus Christ, in the heavenly throne room (Eph 2:6), I now look down beneath my feet into the kingdom of the air: the kingdom of darkness, and declare to you Satan, every ruling principality, magistrate, power and demon. I bind your power over me, and demand*

that you depart my soul, my home and my environment, in the Name of Jesus Christ of Nazareth, and through his blood shed for me, according to the Word of Elohiym -- the Living God -- [Father, Son and Holy Spirit] (Mt 16:19; 12:29; Lk 10:19).

9. **Cleansing of Sexual Sins:** When lust, sexual perversion and/or deviancy have been manifest in your life, pray the following: *"Now that the demons of the powers darkness in the heavenlies are bound, in the Name of Jesus Christ, I hereby cut off their communication, power and influence, to accuse or harass me personally or in and through and human being. Specifically, I take authority over demonic spirits of lust, sexual perversion and deviancy, sexual fantasies, masturbation, homosexuality, adultery, fornication and unclean thoughts. I bind you and break your power over me, my spouse, and my children (when applicable). I command you to leave my soul, my home and my environment, and become part of the footstool of Jesus Christ (Heb 1:13 & 10:13), until you are destroyed in the lake of fire at the end-time (Rev 20:14-15).*

10. **Cleansing for Addictions:** When alcohol, drugs or other forms of addiction and/or abuse have been manifest in your life, pray the following: *"I take authority over demonic spirits of bondage and addiction to (--name them --). I bind you and break your power over me, my spouse, and my children (when applicable). I command you to leave my soul, my home and my environment, and become part of the footstool of Jesus Christ (Heb 1:13 & 10:13), until you are destroyed in the lake of fire at the end-time (Rev 20:14-15). Through the power of Indwelling Holy Spirit, I will henceforth say "NO" to these things and "YES" to the indwelling presence of God [Elohiym] (Father, Holy Spirit and Jesus Christ, Son of God and of Man).*

11. **Cleansing Negative Emotions:** When fear, anger, rage, family abuse and violence, rejection, self-pity, self-hatred, guilt and shame, inadequacy, unworthiness, jealousy, anxiety and depression, inferiority and insecurity have been manifest in your life, pray the following: *"I take authority over demonic spirits of (--name them --). I bind you and break your power over me, my spouse, and my children (when applicable). I command you to leave my soul, my home and my environment, and become part of the footstool of Jesus Christ (Heb 1:13 & 10:13), until you are destroyed in the lake of fire at the end-time (Rev 20:14-15).*

I henceforth look to Jesus, author and finisher of my salvation, for my identity, approval and validation.

12. **Healing Mental Problems:** When mental and/or emotional problems -- such as anxiety and depression, confusion, doubt, indecision, loss of memory, mental torment, harassing inner voices, laziness and apathy, greed and compromise have been manifest in your life, pray the following: *"I take authority over demonic spirits of (--name them --). I bind you and break your power over me, my spouse, and my children (when applicable). I command you to leave my soul, my home and my environment, and become part of the footstool of Jesus Christ (Heb 1:13 & 10:13), until you are destroyed in the lake of fire at the end-time (Rev 20:14-15). By faith in my Lord and Savior, Jesus Christ, I lay hold of the promise, "For God hath not given us the spirit of fear, but of power, and of love, and of a sound mind" (2 Ti 1:7).*

13. **Deliverance from Demonic Behavior:** When demons of lying, manipulation, cursing, vulgar speech, criticism, mocking, gossiping, prejudice, sophistication, judging, or idle talk have been manifest in your life, pray the following: *"I take authority over demonic spirits of (--name them --). I bind you and break your power over me, my spouse, and my children (when applicable). I command you to leave my soul, my home and my environment, and become part of the footstool of Jesus Christ (Heb 1:13 & 10:13), until you are destroyed in the lake of fire at the end-time (Rev 20:14-15).*

14. **Physical Deliverance:** When demons contributing to physical malfunctions, infirmities, chronic sickness and disease have been manifest in your life, pray the following: *"I take authority over demonic spirits of (--name each of them --). I bind you and break your power over me, my spouse, and my children (when applicable). I command you to leave my soul, my home and my environment, and become part of the footstool of Jesus Christ (Heb 1:13 & 10:13), until you are destroyed in the lake of fire at the end-time (Rev 20:14-15). I hereby embrace the fact that my Lord and Savior, Jesus Christ, took every disease, illness and impairment to the cross (Is 53:4), 'desires above all things that I might enjoy good health' (3 Jn 2); and gave his disciples power to expel demons and heal (Lk 10:9 & 32).*

15. **As a 'cover-all prayer',** pray the following: "*In the Name of Jesus Christ of Nazareth, I hereby take authority over any and every other spirit not of God. I bind you and break your power over me, my spouse, and my children (when applicable). I command you to leave my soul, my home and my environment, and become part of the footstool of Jesus Christ (Heb 1:13 & 10:13), until you are destroyed in the lake of fire at the end-time (Rev 20:14-15). I hereby confess my sole allegiance to the God Almighty, God of Abraham, Isaac and Jacob; and confess that Jesus Christ -- God Who came in the flesh -- is my Lord and Savior; and confess that I have invited God, Holy Spirit, to indwell my spirit, and write on the walls of my heart, the laws of God (Jer 31:33; Heb 8:10; 10:16).*

16. **Ask God to Commission Ministering Angels:** *Father God, Lord Jesus and Holy Spirit, that I might indeed love and worship You with all my heart (spirit) and all my soul, and all my body, I ask you to send forth ministering spirits to minister healing -- body, soul and spirit -- that I might be all You designed me to be; and in faith that You have heard my prayer and have answered it, I ascribe to You all majesty and give you all my honor and glory and praise. I embrace Your promise that if I confess publicly that Jesus, my Lord and Savior is God in the flesh, and trust in him, whom the Father has raised, You will deliver me from the powers of darkness, heal me and lift me up (Rom 10:9-10).*

17. **Maintaining your healing** through your positive confession. *"Whoso offereth praise glorifieth me: and to him that ordereth his conversation aright will I show the salvation of God"* (Ps 50:23). *"A man's belly shall be satisfied with the fruit of his mouth; and with the increase of his lips shall he be filled. Death and life are in the power of the tongue: and they that love it shall eat the fruit thereof"* (Pro 18:20-21). We must not only claim God's promises, we must also learn to speak or confess God's Word daily. We must confess our faith in God's Word. We must not confess lack, as the Heavenly Father has given us everything we need. We must not confess defeat, since God has made us more than conquerors. We must not confess doubt, as it is God Who has given us His faith. We are to speak aloud the things that the Word of God declares as truth. We commonly quote what men have to say on a subject, many times believing them even though they conflict with the Word of God. At the same time, we are often hesitant to quote what God says because demons have convinced us that to do so, we would be lying!

Demons encourage us to concentrate on our circumstances rather than focus on God's Word. Circumstances and situations are subject to change. In fact, one of the things that can cause them to change, is our own confession of God's Word concerning that matter. The Word of God tells us to confess or talk about the things we are believing God to do in our lives and He will bring it to pass (Ps 37:4-5).

For example: *"He (Abraham) staggered not at the promise of God through unbelief; but was strong in faith, giving glory to God; And being fully persuaded that, what he had promised, he was able also to perform. And therefore it was imputed to him for righteousness"* (Rom 4:20-22). God honored his faith. *"(As it is written, I have made thee a father of many nations,) before him whom he believed, even God, who quickeneth the dead, and calleth those things which be not as though they were"* (Rom 4:17).

In contrast to Abraham's confession of faith, we often give in to the suggestion of demons. When in need of finances, the demons try to get us to confess things such as, *"I guess we will just have to take out bankruptcy since there is no way we can pay our bills,"* or *"I have no idea how we will be able to make our house payment."* Instead, we need to align our confession with the Word of God. *"My God shall supply all your (my) need according to his riches in glory by Christ Jesus"* (Phil 4:19)

"But seek ye first the kingdom of God, and his righteousness; and all these things shall be added unto you (me)" (Matthew 6:33). (Emphasis ours). We should confess our faith and trust in the Lord by saying, *"I don't know how the Lord is going to help me meet this particular need, but I confess that He will because He cares for me."* *"Casting all your cares upon Him, for He cares for you"* (1 Pe 5:7).

We manifest -- or bring into reality -- either evil or good, based on what we speak. Jesus referred to this, saying: *"O generation of vipers, how can ye, being evil, speak good things? for out of the abundance of the heart the mouth speaketh. A good man out of the good treasure of the heart bringeth forth good things: and an evil man out of the evil treasure bringeth forth evil things.*

But I say unto you, That every idle word that men shall speak, they shall give account thereof in the day of judgment. For by thy words thou shalt be justified, and by thy words thou shalt be condemned" (Mt 12:34-37). As a Christian -- a child of God -- we should never again confess any of the things that are against God's Word and will.

My Never Again List:
Read the following, marking all those that apply, and adding others as appropriate, to your personal list of negative confessions that, by the grace of God, you will never again speak out, or confess to others, or to yourself – in your inner-dialogue:

[ ]   Never again will I confess "I can't" for *"I can do all things through Christ which strengtheneth me"* (Phil 4:13).

[ ]   Never again will I confess lack, for *"My God shall supply all of my needs according to His riches in glory by Christ Jesus"* (Phil 4:19).

[ ]   Never again will I confess fear, for *"God hath not given us the spirit of fear; but of power, and of love, and of a sound mind"* (2 Ti 1:7).

[ ]   Never again will I confess doubt and lack of faith, for *"God hath dealt to every man the measure of faith"* (Rom 12:3).

[ ]   Never again will I confess weakness, for *"The Lord is the strength of my life"* (Ps 27:1). *"The people that know their God shall be strong and do exploits"* (Dan 11:32).

[ ]   Never again will I confess supremacy of Satan over my life, for *"Greater is He that is within me than he that is in the world"* (1 Jn 4:4).

[ ]   Never again will I confess defeat, for *"God always causeth me to triumph in Christ Jesus"* (2 Cor 2:14).

[ ]   Never again will I confess lack of wisdom, for *"Christ Jesus is made unto me wisdom from God"* (1 Cor 1:30).

[ ]   Never again will I confess sickness, for *"With His stripes I am healed" (Isaiah 53:5). Jesus "Himself took my infirmities and bare my sickness"* (Mt 8:17).

[ ]   Never again will I confess worries and frustrations, for I am *"Casting all my cares upon Him, who careth for me"* (1Pe 5:7). In Christ I am "carefree."

[ ]   Never again will I confess addiction or bondage, for *"Where the Spirit of the Lord is, there is liberty"* (2 Cor 3:17).

[ ]   Never again will I confess condemnation, for *"There is therefore now no condemnation to them which are in Christ Jesus"* (Rom 8:1). I am in Christ; therefore, I am free from condemnation.

[ ]   Never again will I confess loneliness, Jesus said, *"Lo, I am with you always, even unto the end of the world"* (Mt 28:20). He promised, *"I will never leave thee, nor forsake thee"* (Heb 13:5).

[ ]   Never again will I confess curses or bad luck, for *"Christ hath redeemed us from the curse of the law, being made a curse for us. ... that the blessing of Abraham might come on the Gentiles through Jesus Christ; that we might receive the promise of the Spirit through faith"* (Gal 3:13-14).

[ ]   Never again will I confess discontent because *"I have learned, in whatsoever state (circumstances) I am, therewith to be content"* (Phil 4:11).

[ ]   Never again will I confess unworthiness because *"He hath made Him to be sin for us who knew no sin; that we might be made the righteousness of God in Him"* (2 Cor 5:21).

[ ]   Never again will I confess mental illness, *"For God hath not given us the spirit of fear; but of power, and of love, and of a sound mind"* (2 Ti 1:7).

[ ]   _____

The confession of our mouths will eventually manifest, or bring forth, the things we speak out.

When baby Christians, who have not yet learned this truth, God, in His grace, does not give us the things we confess or speak wrongly because they are not in accord with His will. We have not yet learned His will. He looks on our heart, and because we are genuinely desiring to do the will of the Father, He cancels those things that are not His will – our hearts (spirits & souls) are speaking louder than our mouths.

"Lord, who shall abide in thy tabernacle? who shall dwell in thy holy hill? He that walketh uprightly, and worketh righteousness, and speaketh the truth in his heart" (Ps 15:1-2). Moreover, *"ye have not received the spirit of bondage again to fear; but ye have received the Spirit of adoption, whereby we cry, Abba, Father. [And] The Spirit itself beareth witness with our spirit"* (Rom 8:15-16). Since Holy Spirit indwells our spirit, writing God's laws therein, as we continue to speak truth in our hearts, our mouths will soon begin to line up with our hearts. Until that time the Lord is gracious to us when our hearts and our mouths are not agreeing.

Guarding Your Heart (Spirit):

Solomon warned: *"Above all else, guard your heart, for it is the wellspring of life"* (Prov 4:23). Following up on this, we would like to address an area related to the subject of watching our confessions. We should neither agree with, nor allow to go unchallenged, negative things either spoken or written by, or to us by others, since this gives the enemy a doorway into our lives. Examples of this include: e-mail address names and nicknames used by some Christians that are not only very negative but some are actually demonic. Please pray about correcting this if your nickname or e-mail address does not glorify the Lord, as this is a form of an evil confession about yourself.

Be on guard concerning what others confess about you. Remember, *"That if two of you shall agree on earth as touching any thing that they shall ask, it shall be done for them of my Father which is in heaven"* (Mt 18:19). When someone else speaks out, or writes, a negative confession concerning you, renounce it in your heart; and deal with them in love. While it should be our goal to correct their view of us – if possible – remember that your identity is in Christ, not in them. We must stay focused on the fact that the highest law is the law of love. Thus, we should not nag at others, but pray for them. Certainly, we can gently correct those who share the same spiritual knowledge we do, since they are usually eager to overcome in this area. However, for those who have never been taught concerning this, it is wisdom to just pray for them until they come to the knowledge of the truth.

Finally, when it comes to our confessions, it is important that we get our eyes off of self and focused on God. The power of positive confession is often abused when one's confessions focus on their own needs for material things, their own health, etc. Many are heard claiming cars, property, houses, perfect health in a sin-ridden world, etc., but seldom are these same folk heard claiming God's promises for the salvation of the souls of their fellowman.

We should be certain our priorities are right when claiming and confessing. For example, we often hear people confessing the first half of the following verse, which completely misses its intent. *"Beloved, I wish above all things that thou mayest prosper and be in health, **even as thy soul prospereth**"* (3 John 2). The Lord's greatest desire is for us to grow in Him, enabling us to bring others to the knowledge of His mercy, grace and love. When we are not stressing this in our confessions, we are being led astray by demons.

Chapter Ten ~ Engaging the Enemy

Review:

Thus far, we have been focused on our preparation for engaging in spiritual warfare. This preparation has included:

- The cleansing and preparation of body, soul and spirit;
- Adorning ourselves in the proper uniform;
- Selecting the proper personal weapons;
- Receiving proper warfare capabilities through spiritual gifts that are bestowed by Holy Spirit;
- Operating in liaison with God's holy angels, who bring to bear spiritual armament.
- Preparing for combat.

Once we have successfully completed these assignments, we are prepared to engage the enemy. However, there is one thing we may not have taken into consideration – the enemy has assigned spies who have become familiar with our talents and tactics; our strengths and strategies; as well as our weaknesses. Thus, if we are to wage a winning war, it is incumbent on us – the church – to give due diligence to spying out the enemy. One of the first things any military spy is concerned with is the organization of the enemy forces. The prophet John, having been given a vision of the end-times, declared, *"I saw the beast and the kings of the earth and their armies, gathered together to make war against the rider on the horse [Yeshua Messiah] and his army"* (Rev 19:19-20).

The apostle Paul, preparing us for this battle, said: *" Use all the armor and weaponry that God provides, so that you will be able to stand against the deceptive tactics of the Adversary. **For we are not struggling against human beings, but against the rulers, authorities and cosmic powers governing this darkness, against the spiritual forces of evil in the heavenly realm**. So take up every piece of war equipment God provides; so that when the evil day comes, you will be able to resist; and when the battle is won, you will still be standing"* (Eph 6:11-14 CJB).

Paul, in an effort to prepare the church for this coming battle, described briefly the organization of the enemy's forces that are aligned against us – principalities, ruling authorities and cosmic forces. Principalities are spiritual (demonic) princes governing municipalities, regions or areas; ruling authorities are demonic entities assigned to rule over those demons engaged in specific warfare strategies, and the cosmic forces are those demons operating under the direction of these ruling authorities to carry out their demonic – spiritual – warfare.

The Spiritual Battle we are engaged in is a battle between God's Kingdom of Light and Righteousness; and Satan's Kingdom of Darkness and Wickedness. The weaponry used in this warfare is a war of words: the declaration of truth, blessings and righteousness, vs., lies, curses and wickedness. The battle involves an intense struggle – a life or death struggle – between ourselves and unseen powers of evil. It could be a frightful thing, were it not for one thing: We have been promised protection; and have already been declared the winners! But, before we get ahead of ourselves, let's look at what Scripture says.

Key Scripture ~ This Scripture is truly the key to our understanding the spiritual battle we are in; our role in this battle; and the organized structure of the Adversary's forces of evil. As you take time to read through the following translations, these keys should become apparent.

"We wrestle not against flesh and blood, but against principalities, against powers, against the rulers of the darkness of this world, against spiritual wickedness in high places" (Eph 6:12 KJV).

"We are not struggling against human beings, but against the rulers, authorities and cosmic powers governing this darkness, against the spiritual forces of evil in the heavenly realm" (Eph 6:12 CJB).

"We are not fighting against humans. We are fighting against forces and authorities and against rulers of darkness and powers in the spiritual world" (Eph 6:12 CEV).

"We are not wrestling with flesh and blood [contending only with physical opponents], but against the despotisms, against the powers, against [the master spirits who are] the world rulers of this present darkness, against the spirit forces of wickedness in the heavenly (supernatural) sphere" (Eph 6:12 AMP).

"Our struggle is not against flesh and blood, but against the rulers, against the powers, against the world forces of this darkness, against the spiritual forces of wickedness in the heavenly places" (Eph 6:12 NASB).

"Our fight is not against human beings. It is against the rulers, the authorities and the powers of this dark world. It is against the spiritual forces of evil in the heavenly world" (Eph 6:12 NirV).

"Our struggle is not against blood and flesh, but against principalities, against authorities, against the universal lords of this darkness, against spiritual [power] of wickedness in the heavenlies" (Eph 6:12 Darby). … *"Our wrestling is not against blood and flesh, but against the principalities, against the authorities, against the world rulers of this darkness, against spirit forces of perniciousness in the heavenly places"* (Eph 6:12 Wuest). …
"This is no afternoon athletic contest that we'll walk away from and forget about in a couple of hours. This is for keeps, a life-or-death fight to the finish against the Devil and all his angels" (Eph 6:12 THE MESSAGE).

Now that you have reviewed the key Scripture, as rendered in a number of different translations, let's reexamine the keys mentioned:

1. We are – as mentioned in The Message – in a 'for-keeps', 'life-or-death' 'fight to the finish!'

2. Our struggle is not against other human beings – we are engaged in a spirit to spirit battle – our spirit against the fallen spirits.

3. Our role is that of a gladiator – fighting for our life: not just this life, but our eternal life.

4. Our Adversary is well organized – having under his command: Principalities [or Despots]; Rulers [Powers, Authorities, Master Spirits or Warlords]; and Cosmic Forces [Spirit Forces of Perniciousness, Spiritual Forces of Evil.]

5. The battle-field covers a vast expanse – the supernatural – the heavenly realms and the dark (unseen), dimension of this fallen earth.]

This could seem overwhelming and hopeless, were it not for God's Word that precedes our key text. Let's read it from the Message Translation, which is one of the more graphic: *"That about wraps it up. God is strong, and he wants you strong. So take everything the Master has set out for you, well-made weapons of the best materials. And put them to use so you will be able to stand up to everything the Devil throws your way"* (Eph 6:10-12 THE MESSAGE).

The Dark Domain:
In previous chapters, we have pretty well covered all but No. 4 of the identified aspects of this supernatural – fight to the finish – battle. That aspect described in number 4 – is the Dark Domain [the domain of spirit beings and its organization.] To fully comprehend this domain we need to understand its place in the cosmos.

Scripture identifies the battleground of this war as being in 'heavenly places,' yet even this can be a bit confusing. The word translated 'heaven' is the plural form of the Hebrew word, *'shamayim'* – or the Greek word, *'ouranoi.'* Understanding this does not provide a complete answer, since there are three different heavens mentioned in Scripture.

1. **The first heaven** ~ is that of our atmosphere – where we live and where the birds fly: *"God said, ... **let birds fly above the earth across the face of the firmament of the heavens"*** (Gen 1:20) ... *"**The birds of the heavens** have their home; They sing among the branches"* (Ps 104:12). ... *"The God of heaven has given you a kingdom, power, strength, and glory; and wherever the children of men dwell, or the beasts of the field and the **birds of the heaven**, He has given them into your hand, and has made you ruler over them all"* (Dan 2:37-38).

2. **The Mid-Heaven** ~ alco called the second heaven, is where angels – both the righteous and the wicked fly, deliver messages, minister to, or oppress, mankind, and engage in battle: *"There was a **great red dragon** with seven heads and ten horns, and ... **its tail swept a third of the stars out of heaven and threw them down to the earth**. **It stood in front of the woman [the church] about to give birth, so that it might devour the child the moment it was born**.* "She gave birth to a son, a male child, the one who will rule all the nations with a staff of iron. But her child was snatched up to God and his throne; and she fled into the desert, where she has a place prepared by God so that she can be taken care of for 1,260 days.

    *"**Next there was a battle in heaven — Michael and his angels fought against the dragon, and the dragon and his angels fought back.** But it was not strong enough to win, so that there was no longer any place for them in heaven. The great dragon was thrown out, that ancient serpent, also known as **the Devil and Satan [the Adversary], the deceiver of the whole world. He was hurled down to the earth, and his angels were hurled down with him.**

    *"Then I heard a loud voice in heaven saying, "**Now have come God's victory, power and kingship, and the authority of his Messiah; because the Accuser of our brothers, who accuses them day and night before God, has been thrown out!** "They defeated him because of the Lamb's blood and because of the message of their witness.** Even when facing death they did not cling to life. Therefore, rejoice, heaven and you who live there! But woe to you, land and sea, for the Adversary has come down to you, and he is very angry, because*

he knows that his time is short!" (Rev 12:3-12 CJB).

*"Next **I saw another angel flying in mid-heaven** with everlasting Good News to proclaim to those living on the earth – to every nation, tribe, language and people. **In a loud voice he said, "Fear God, give him glory, for the hour has come when he will pass judgment***!

"Worship the One who made heaven and earth, the sea and the springs of water!" **Another angel, a second one, followed, saying, "She has fallen! She has fallen! Babylon the Great***! She made all the nations drink the wine of God's fury caused by her whoring!. **Another angel, a third one, followed them and said in a loud voice, "If anyone worships the beast and its image and receives the mark on his forehead or on his hand, he will indeed drink the wine of God's fury poured undiluted into the cup of his rage***" (Rev 14:6-10 CJB).

3. **The Third heaven** ~ where Father God dwells – and where a few humans have been "caught up." Enoch was apparently one of the first: *"When Enoch was sixty-five, he had a son named Methuselah, and during the next three hundred years he had more children. **Enoch truly loved God, and God took him away** at the age of three hundred sixty-five"* (Gen 5:21-23). ... *"**Enoch had faith and did not die**. He pleased God, and **God took him up to heaven**. That's why his body was never found"* (Heb 11:5 CEV).

Then, there was Moses, who – although he experienced death, he appeared with Jesus and Elijah on the Mount of Transfiguration. *"Moses climbed Mount Nebo from the plains of Moab to the top of Pisgah, across from Jericho. There the Lord showed him the whole land ... Then the Lord said to him, "This is the land I promised on oath to Abraham, Isaac and Jacob when I said, 'I will give it to your descendants.' I have let you see it with your eyes, but you will not cross over into it." And Moses the servant of the Lord died there in Moab, as the Lord had said. He buried him in Moab, in the valley opposite Beth Peor, but to this day no one knows where his grave is"* (Deut 34:1 & 4-6 NIV).

"After six days Jesus took Peter, James and John with him and led them up a high mountain, where they were all alone. There he was transfigured before them. His clothes became dazzling white, whiter than anyone in the world could bleach them. And there appeared before them Elijah and Moses, who were talking with Jesus" (Mark 9:2-4 NIV).

161

Elijah was another: *"Suddenly, as they were walking on and talking, there appeared a fiery chariot with horses of fire; and as it separated the two of them from each other, **Elijah went up into heaven** in a whirlwind. Elisha saw it and cried out, "My father! My father!"* (2 Kings 2:11-12 CJB). ... Stephen, as he was being stoned to death for his witness, was blessed beyond measure to see Jesus and Father God witnessing his martyrdom: *"But he, **full of the Holy Spirit, looked up to heaven and saw God's Shekinah Glory, with Yeshua Messiah standing at the right hand of God**. "Look!" he exclaimed, "I see heaven opened and the Son of Man standing at the right hand of God!"* (Acts 7:55-56 CJB).

Paul, or the person whom he was referring to, was "caught up" to: **"I know a man in union with the Messiah who fourteen years ago was snatched up to the third heaven; whether he was in the body or outside the body I don't know, God knows.** *And I know that such a man – whether in the body or apart from the body I don't know, God knows – was snatched into Gan-Eden and heard things that cannot be put into words, things unlawful for a human being to utter"* (2 Cor 12:2-5 CJB).

4. John, the Revelator, seems to have experienced this also, for he wrote: *"After this I looked and there before me was a great multitude that no one could count, from every nation, tribe, people and language, standing before the throne and in front of the Lamb. ... All the angels were standing around the throne and around the elders and the four living creatures. ... Then one of the elders asked me, "These in white robes — who are they, and where did they come from?" I answered, "Sir, you know." And he said, "These are they who have come out of the great tribulation; they have washed their robes and made them white in the blood of the Lamb"* (Rev 7:9-15 NIV).

The Spiritual Realms:
The Bible actually identifies eight spiritual dimensions or realms:

1. That realm **Above the Heavens** ~ Where God's glory dwells, and where Satan apparently dwelled before his rebellion and fall (Ps 8:1; 108:4-5; Eph 1:20; 4:10; Isa 14:12-14).

2. The Third Heaven ~ Where God's Throne of Grace is – where Paul visited and heard holy things (2 Cor 2:12). [See references above]

3. The Second Heaven ~ or mid heaven – where the spiritual battle rages. [See references above]

4. The First Heaven ~ Where the birds fly – and where Satan dwells as the Prince of the Powers of the Air, since his fall. [See references above]

5. The Face of the Earth ~ *The* place of human habitation – also where the demons under Satan's command, prowl like roaring lions, seeking whom they may devour. *["From one person **God made all nations who live on earth**, and **He decided when and where every nation would be**" (Acts 17:26 CEV). ... "Be on your guard and stay awake. **Your enemy, the devil, is like a roaring lion, sneaking around to find someone to attack**. But you must resist the devil and stay strong in your faith. You know that all over the world the Lord's followers are suffering just as you are" (1 Peter 5:8-10 CEV).]*

6. The Grave, The Sea, The Deep ~ The burial place for human bodies. Our physical bodies cannot inhabit the spiritual realm. *"I declare to you, brothers, that flesh and blood cannot inherit the kingdom of God, nor does the perishable inherit the imperishable"* (1 Cor 15:50-51); Describing live on earth, Job declared: *"As a cloud vanishes and is gone, so he who goes down to the grave does not return. He will never come to his house again; his place will know him no more"* (Job 7:9-10). But, as God's redeemed children, we have His promise for a life hereafter. *"God will redeem my life from the grave; he will surely take me to himself"* (Ps 49:15).

The apostle Paul wrote: *"Listen, I tell you a mystery: We will not all sleep, but we will all be changed – in a flash, in the twinkling of an eye, at the last trumpet. For the trumpet will sound, the dead will be raised imperishable, and we will be changed. For the perishable must clothe itself with the imperishable, and the mortal with immortality. When the perishable has been clothed with the imperishable, and the mortal with immortality, then the saying that is written will come true: "Death has been swallowed up in victory"* (1 Cor 15:51-54).

7. The Abyss, Sheol, The Netherworld, the Bottomless Pit ~
*"I will make the nations quake at the sound of its fall when I **cast it down to Sheol** with those who descend into the pit, and all the trees of Eden, the choice and best of Lebanon, all [the trees] that drink water, will be comforted in the **netherworld** [at Assyria's downfall]. They also shall go down into **Sheol** with it to those who were slain by the sword — yes, those who were its arm, who dwelt under its shadow in the midst of the nations. To whom [O Egypt] among the trees of Eden are you thus like in glory and in greatness? Yet you [also] shall be brought down with the trees of Eden to the **netherworld**"* (Ezek 31:16-18 AMP).

163

"Son of man, wail over the multitude of Egypt and cast them down, even her and the daughters of the famous and majestic nations, to the **netherworld***, with those who go down to* **the pit***; ... The strong among the mighty shall speak of [Pharaoh] out of the midst of* **Sheol (the place of the dead, the netherworld)** *with those who helped him; they are gone down; they lie still, even the uncircumcised (the heathen) slain by the sword. Whose graves are set in* **the uttermost parts of the pit** *and whose company is round about her grave, all of them slain, fallen by the sword, who caused terror to spread in the land of the living. Elam [an auxiliary of Assyria] is there and all her multitude round about her grave, all of them slain, fallen by the sword, who have gone down uncircumcised into* **the netherworld***, who caused their terror to spread in the land of the living and have borne their shame with those who go down to* **the pit***. And they shall not lie with the mighty who have fallen of the uncircumcised [and] who have gone down to* **Sheol (the place of the dead, the netherworld)** *with their weapons of war, whose swords were laid [with honors] under their heads and whose iniquities are upon their bones, for they caused their terror to spread in the land of the living"* (Ezek 32:18 – 27 AMP).

8. The Lake of Fire ~ *"The beast and the false prophet were both thrown alive into* **the lake of fire that burns with sulfur"** (Rev 19:20-21 CJB). ... *"The devil, who deceived them, was thrown into* **the lake of burning sulfur,** *where the beast and the false prophet had been thrown"* (Rev 20:10). ... *"Then death and Hades were* **thrown into the lake of fire. The lake of fire is the second death.** *If anyone's name was not found written in the book of life, he was* **thrown into the lake of fire"** (Rev 20:14-15). ... This was prophesied long ago. The prophet Isaiah declared: *"The Lord will cause men to hear his majestic voice and will make them see his arm coming down with raging anger and consuming fire"* (Isa 30:30).

Sodom and Gomorrah – cities God destroyed due to their wickedness – were consumed with such heat, that the area, once a hill country, now lies beneath the Dead Sea. And God's Word declares: *"Sodom and Gomorrah and the surrounding towns gave themselves up to sexual immorality and perversion. They serve as an example of those who suffer the punishment of eternal fire"* (Jude 7). Each of these eight dimensions plays a significant role in this drama of the ages – this spiritual warfare in the cosmos. However, due to our fallen nature, we can only observe – with our physical eyes – those things taking place within the first heaven: the earth and the canopy of air surrounding it. Depicting all of the dimensions graphically is impossible, but the following provides a rough idea.

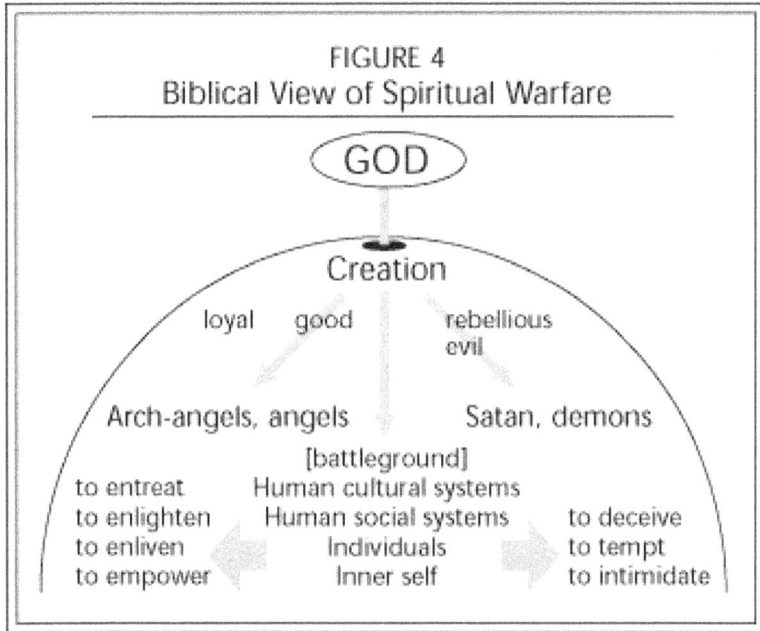

FIGURE 4
Biblical View of Spiritual Warfare

However, while we are limited in our physical senses to beholding only those things within the first heaven, we may – when spiritually awakened, with our spiritual eyes opened – be aware of, and occasionally even see, spiritual beings operating within the other dimensions. We as born-again believers in Yeshua Messiah, are, after all, seated with him in the heavenly realm (Eph 2:6). Seated there with him, we may look down, overlooking in a sense, the entirety of this great spiritual conflagration. We will speak of this, and its impact on our ability to achieve success a bit later, but first, we need to examine Satan's counterfeit kingdom – a counterfeit to God's kingdom here on earth.

Satan's Counterfeit Kingdom:
Satan is a master counterfeiter, and those who worship him – who are members of his kingdom, are deceived. *"The lawless one ... whom the Lord Jesus will overthrow with the breath of his mouth and destroy by the splendor of his coming, will be in accordance with the work of Satan displayed in all kinds of counterfeit miracles, signs and wonders, and in every sort of evil that deceives those who are perishing. They perish because they refused to love the truth and so be saved. For this reason God sends them a powerful delusion so that they will believe the lie and so that all will be condemned who have not believed the truth but have delighted in wickedness"* (2 Thess 2:8-12).

165

Satan's vast counterfeit kingdom began in the primeval ages past, and was, for a time, interrupted by Noah's Flood. However, shortly thereafter, it was reestablished, its headquarters in Babel, its earthly pawns and leaders, Nimrod and Semiramis – King and Queen of Babylon. Nimrod and Semiramis who are well known for the construction of the Tower of Babel and the founding of the city-state of Babel, are less well known as founders of the ancient "Mystery Religion" described in Revelation.

"Then the angel carried me away in the Spirit into a desert. There I saw a woman sitting on a scarlet beast that was covered with blasphemous names and had seven heads and ten horns. The woman was dressed in purple and scarlet, and was glittering with gold, precious stones and pearls. She held a golden cup in her hand, filled with abominable things and the filth of her adulteries. This title was written on her forehead:

MYSTERY
BABYLON THE GREAT
THE MOTHER OF PROSTITUTES
AND OF THE ABOMINATIONS OF THE EARTH"
(Rev 17:3-5).

This worldwide kingdom commenced with the founders of Babel – Nimrod and Semiramis – who were among the second invasion of the Nephilim (giants). As nephilim – crossbreeds between humans and the watchers [fallen angels (Gen 6)], they were committed to destroy humankind, beginning with all the descendants of Shem. It was Shem's descendants whom God had declared through the prophetic voice of Noah, to be the lineage of the coming Deliverer.

In our book, "Mysteries of the Bible: The Primeval Era" we discuss in detail the nephilim, the establishment of this evil kingdom, and the mystery religions, which have spread from this inauspicious beginning, to encompass the whole earth. Today, members of the occult – which means 'hidden' – are, knowingly or unknowingly, aligned with the Great Mystery Religion [Babylon the Great: Mother of Prostitutes (false religions); and are – in God's eyes -- the abomination of the whole earth.

Satan's followers – those in the occult – have; being under the delusion identified in the foregoing Scripture; and no doubt enticed by Satan himself; conceptualized a kingdom that counterfeits the eight dimensions or realms within the Kingdom of God. To grasp in full the scope of the spiritual battle we are engaged in, we will look at the eight dimensions in Satan's counterfeit kingdom.

Satan's Kingdom of Darkness:
Satan, being the arch-counterfeiter, has designed a kingdom – the kingdom of darkness in the heavens – with seven dimensions, imitating the concept of seven being representative of perfection, by counterfeiting the seven dimensions of the kingdom of God.

The Seventh Dimension ~ The seventh dimension of Satan's kingdom is but a delusion – Satan's own delusion. We read about this in the Old Testament prophetic book of Isaiah. *"How you have fallen from heaven, O morning star, son of the dawn! You have been cast down to the earth, you who once laid low the nations!* **You said in your heart, "I will ascend to heaven; I will raise my throne above the stars of God; I will sit enthroned on the mount of assembly, on the utmost heights of the sacred mountain. I will ascend above the tops of the clouds; I will make myself like the Most High"** (Isa 14:12-14).

What an absurd delusion – that a created being – any created being – could even dream of elevating himself above God – above the pre-existent, eternal, uncreated deity of the universe! How, you might be asking, could one created by the uncreated, ever come to envision such at thing? Here is the answer, provided by God himself, through the prophet Ezekiel:

"This is what the Sovereign Lord says: 'You were the model of perfection, full of wisdom and perfect in beauty. You were in Eden, the garden of God; every precious stone adorned you: ruby, topaz and emerald, chrysolite, onyx and jasper, sapphire, turquoise and beryl. Your settings and mountings were made of gold; on the day you were created they were prepared. You were anointed as a guardian cherub, for so I ordained you. You were on the holy mount of God; you walked among the fiery stones. You were blameless in your ways from the day you were created till wickedness was found in you. ... **Your heart grew proud because of your beauty, you corrupted your wisdom for the sake of your splendor"** (Ezek 28:12-15 & 17).

"Instead you are brought down to Sheol, to the uttermost depths of the pit. Those who see you will stare at you, reflecting on what has become of you: 'Is this the man who shook the earth, who made kingdoms tremble, who made the world a desert, who destroyed its cities, who would not set his prisoners free?' "All other kings of the nations, all of them, lie in glory, each in his tomb. But you are discarded, unburied, like a loathed branch, clothed like the slain who were pierced by the sword, then fall to the stones inside a pit, like a corpse to be trampled underfoot.

You will not be joined with those kings in the grave, because you destroyed your own land, you have brought death to your own people. [Even] the descendants of [these] evildoers will be utterly forgotten" (Isa 14:12-20 CJB).

It was apparently to that position in space, where he aspired to establish his throne, that Satan took Jesus to tempt him – showing him all the kingdoms of the earth [all of the occult kingdoms that have followed Babylon's model – setting up a false religion; including the worship of demons.] *"The Adversary took him up to the summit of a very high mountain, showed him all the kingdoms of the world in all their glory, and said to him, "All this I will give you if you will bow down and worship me." "Away with you, Satan!" Yeshua told him, "For Scripture says, 'Worship Adonai your God, and serve only him"* (Matt 4:8-10 CJB).

It was from this high place, after being tempted by Satan that Yeshua Messiah [Jesus Christ] responded, offering a direct challenge: *"Worship Adonai your God, and serve only him."* To comprehend the significance of this challenge, one must understand that Christ is himself Adonai. Thus, his response to this arch-counterfeiter, was essentially a command, directing Satan to bow and worship him! Only when one understands this, does the next verse in Matthew's Gospel – containing Satan's response – reveal its full meaning: *"Then the Adversary let him alone"* (Matt 4:11 CJB).

The Sixth Dimension ~ According to occultists, this dimension is called the Azura Kingdom – and within this kingdom are several planes, regions, sub-regions, zones, etc., ruled by the Archspirit, Sat Kumara. According to them, every mystical act, every wisdom of the unholy, every [witch]craft, is born in Azura and astrally [spiritually] projected, into the five lower dimensions. There are – allegedly – within the Kingdom of Asura, – millions of 'mighty spirits' referred to as the "Guardians of the Flame" (Abhidevanadas). This sixth dimension would seem to correlate with that dimension of the 'principalities' of the kingdom of darkness referenced by the Apostle Paul in Ephesians 6 – being demonic princes commanding all demonic activity within the geographical region they rule over. An example of these principalities is the Prince of Persia, mentioned in Daniel 10:13-20. We will be learning more about these principalities soon, but for now, we will continue our overview of the seven dimensions of Satan's counterfeit kingdom.

The Fifth Dimension ~ This kingdom is the Terrestrial Kingdom [Kingdom of the Heavens]. Within this kingdom, there are –

allegedly – two "Grand Divisions": the Casual World [where everything is born], ruled by the Archspirit, Lord Gotamy; and the Etheric Heavens [the unseen], ruled by Saint Goo-Ling, who – uses advanced manipulation against mankind – which no man can detect; except those who have been delivered by and through the living power of Jesus Christ. Within this kingdom, there are – allegedly – more than thirty-three million (33,000,000) demi-gods, ruled over by the Archspirit, Ba-Vara.

According to the information contained within the works of the occultists, these 'demi-gods' seem to equate to the Ruling Powers mentioned by Paul in Ephesians 6. If so, their number is a gross exaggeration – or the works thus manifest by these demi-gods, is but the beginning of their attack against humanity.

The Fourth Dimension ~ This kingdom, referred to by occultists as the Kingdom of the Air, is also called the Astral Kingdom. It is said to be ruled over by the Archspirit, Lord Sagna [formerly a Deva (a Watcher or Guardian Angel)]. This Archspirit is allegedly in control of billions of Yansdavas [Demons of the Air]; and rules over millions of other Devas and Devatas [male and female Watchers or Guardian Angels], within the realm of Sahasra. There are, within this dimension – allegedly – billions of demons and millions of "guardian spirits."

These demonic entities may correlate with the cosmic forces mentioned by the Apostle Paul. Their activity, according to occultists, is to watch over, or guard, those humans within their kingdom and under their power. The billions of demons and guardian spirits they make reference to, seemingly correlate with the number of humans on the earth. There is also – according to occultists – a Lower Astral Kingdom which they describe as being made up of twenty-six million (26,000,000) individual planes, each covering many regions of the earth. This Astral Kingdom is ruled over by the spirit, King Elam, who is second in command within the Astral Kingdom, and worshipped by those in the occults, as a god.

The Third Dimension ~ This dimension is referred to by occultists. as the Kingdom of Fire. According to adherents to the occults, there are within this dimension, millions of mighty dark angels – angels of death. Again, this dimension is divided into two major planes: The first is Anda, ruled over by the Archangel, Ahankar, who governs innumerable courts, guarded over by Gnomes [Subterranean spirits (demons)]; and the second plane being a place of punishment, ruled by the Archangel, Chita [the Lord of Fire]; designed for those who are physically dead on the earth.

Within this plane, supposedly, lies the Kingdom of Yamalok, ruled by the Archspirit, Lord Naga [Lord of Death and Punishment.] He is said to control millions and millions of mighty dark angels. Paul, while does not provide such detail of the kingdom of darkness, he does infer that it is a well organized demonic kingdom. *"For we are not struggling against human beings, but against the rulers, authorities and cosmic powers governing this darkness, against the spiritual forces of evil in the heavenly realm"* (Eph 6:12 CJB).

The Second Dimension ~ This dimension is also referred to as the Occult, or hidden, Kingdom, or Water Kingdom. Within this kingdom there are – allegedly – five planes or zones: Lumani; Banni; Lemuria; Gamma; and Alantis. Within each of these zones, there is said to be 220 [or 1,100] regions, ruled over by Pritha. Within each region, there are to be 2,000 occult centers [or 440,000 centers]; each ruled by a Huna [Supreme Mermaid] that controls millions of mermaids and water demons. Beneath the water is supposed to be the Banwar Kingdom, ruled by Archspirit, Lord Kaliya, who is androgynous [being neither male nor female]; who lives in an occult underwater city, named Gupha, that is located beneath the Bermuda Triangle [the Zone of Death]. Each of the five planes within this dimension is said to have a great demon [a demi-god with four hands] ruling over it

The First Dimension ~ The First Dimension, according to occultists, is the Kingdom of the Earth. There are, supposedly, ten major zones of spiritual operations governed by the forces of darkness, each ruled over by Arahatha ["Guardian Angels"]. The ten zones are described as follows:
1. *The Gobi Desert and Afghanistan,*
2. *Agam Des in Tibet,*
3. *Himalaya Mountains in India,*
4. *The Forest of Slurping in India,*
5. *Virndavan, a City in India,*
6. *California in the United States [Ruled over by Seth],*
7. *Ibadan, a City in Nigeria,*
8. *Jerusalem in Israel,*
9. *Tabuse, ruling in Japan and around the Great Pyramid in Egypt,*
10. *The Devic Kingdom, ruled by a female Archspirit [a Seraphim] named, Visel, who lives in a spiritual city called, NU, located somewhere in Iran.*

Within each of these ten zones, occultists allege, there are 127 [or 1,270] occult regions, each ruled by Demon Earth-masters which project metaphysical powers into people, to create and/or maintain, secret societies, churches and religious movements; established for the operation of witchcraft, esoteric and related cosmic forces.

170

Within each of these occult regions, there are 3,000 occult centers, through which 30,000,000 Elemental Forces [Gnomes (Supreme Elements)] operate via the mystical AUM vibrations [Mantra Sound Vibrations]; and within each of these centers, there are millions of elemental spirit demons.

Occult Science: The Mystery Religion:
With this background of the Kingdom of Darkness – as understood by its adherents and practitioners – those who believe it to be in the right, and the Kingdom of God to be in the wrong, let's look at the more common occult teachings:

First, there are the Occult Metaphysics [the secret, most confidential aspects of their teachings]; then there are the Mystical Sciences, practiced by Mystical Adepts called, Living Grand Masters. This is the cosmological order of Astral and Terrestrial Hierarchy that are universally recognized in the occult societies. The Exoteric are the public teachings, and an occult adept models the techniques of his master. There are, within their system of religion, spirit entities, demons, de-mi-gods, Arch spirits, Archangels, etc. A Guru is an elevated Spiritual Master.

To become a Grand Master, one must progress through five schools of the occult, each referred to as a Seal. The five seals are identified by the following symbolic numbers: Level 1 – 333; Level 2-- 666; Level 3 – 999; Level 4 – 1330; and Level 5 – 003; operating a total of 400,000 minuet mystical degrees. The seals are awarded according to the numbers of demons the occult individual has learned to control [as if any unregenerate person has control over any demon!] The criteria for earning the seals is as follows:

First Cosmic Seal ~ The 'Devic Seal' symbolized by the number [333] is awarded one who is empowered to control not less than forty thousand (40,000) demons.

Second Cosmic Seal ~ This 'Seal of Kai' symbolized by the number [666] is awarded one who is empowered to control not less than one hundred sixty thousand (160,000) demons. Many well known politicians, military commanders, etc., living today, are said to be at this occult level of operations.

Third Cosmic Seal ~ "This 'Shiva Seal' symbolized by the number [999] is understood as 'The Seal of Destruction.' One who is awarded this seal is an individual empowered to command not less than two million, five hundred thousand (2,500,000) demons; as well as having demonstrated the ability to master one''s own occult and psychic projections.

171

Women are generally kept at this level, with only a few surpassing it.

Fourth Cosmic Seal ~ This is the Terrestrial "Seal of Ba-Vara" symbolized by the number [1330]. One who is awarded this seal is referred to as a "Living Grand Master" of the Order of Astral and Terrestrial **Hierarchy** – being one empowered to command not less than one hundred million (100,000,000) spirits and thirty-three million (33,000,000) de-mi-gods.

This is the level attained by the leaders of many secret societies – those who hold the title of "Grand Master." Some of the organizations bestowing this, or a similar title on their leader include: The Grand Lodge of Freemasons; Knights Templar; Order of the Orange; Order of Hibernians; Knights of Columbus; Mormonism, Presbyters Esoteric Order; The Grange; a number of Lodges, and many others.

Fifth Cosmic Seal ~ This "Seal of Tuzassotama" symbolized by [Liber 003] is one who has met the criteria for, and obtained, all of the other seals; and who is, with the award of this seal, empowered to proclaim himself as "God," "Lord," "Universal Master," or "God-incarnate" on earth – one considered to be capable of controlling all the spirits in all of the occult kingdoms.

Principalities:
Ephesians 6:12 introduces Rulers over various territories and forms of evil: I.e., manipulation, lies, betrayal, sorcery, witchcraft, etc. In these seals described above, we see also an introduction to the Principalities. A principality (or princedom) is a monarchial feudatory or sovereign state, ruled or reigned over by a monarch who holds the title of prince or princess, or (in the widest sense), a monarch using another title that is within the generic concept of the term prince.

Principalities have existed throughout antiquity – even before the kingdoms we are generally familiar with such as Greece, Rome, Persia, etc. Long before these were established, there were many small City-states, known as principalities. Jerusalem – initially called Salem – was one such city-state, comprising only eight and one-half walled-in acres when David captured it. Making it the seat of his kingdom, Jerusalem prospered and grew, later becoming the chief city of the nation of Israel.

Another feudal state which existed at the same time as ancient Israel, and mentioned in Scripture is Persia; and what we are told about it is very relevant to our study.

172

"In the third year of Cyrus king of Persia, a revelation was given to Daniel (who was called Belteshazzar). Its message was true and it concerned a great war. The understanding of the message came to him in a vision.

"At that time I, Daniel, mourned for three weeks. I ate no choice food; no meat or wine touched my lips; and I used no lotions at all until the three weeks were over. On the twenty-fourth day of the first month, as I was standing on the bank of the great river, the Tigris, I looked up and there before me was a man dressed in linen, with a belt of the finest gold around his waist. His body was like chrysolite, his face like lightning, his eyes like flaming torches, his arms and legs like the gleam of burnished bronze, and his voice like the sound of a multitude.

"I, Daniel, was the only one who saw the vision; the men with me did not see it, but such terror overwhelmed them that they fled and hid themselves. So I was left alone, gazing at this great vision; I had no strength left, my face turned deathly pale and I was helpless. Then I heard him speaking, and as I listened to him, I fell into a deep sleep, my face to the ground. A hand touched me and set me trembling on my hands and knees. He said, "Daniel, you who are highly esteemed, consider carefully the words I am about to speak to you, and stand up, for I have now been sent to you."

*"And when he said this to me, I stood up trembling. Then he continued, "Do not be afraid, **Daniel. Since the first day that you set your mind to gain understanding and to humble yourself before your God, your words were heard, and I have come in response to them. But the prince of the Persian kingdom resisted me twenty-one days.** Then Michael, one of the chief princes, came to help me, because **I was detained there with the king of Persia**. Now I have come to explain to you what will happen to your people in the future, for the vision concerns a time yet to come." (Dan 10:1-14). ...*

*"So he said, "Do you know why I have come to you? **Soon I will return to fight against the prince of Persia, and when I go, the prince of Greece will come;** but first I will tell you what is written in the Book of Truth. No one supports me against them except Michael, your prince"* (Dan 10:20-11:1). These Scriptures make it clear that each geographical region – each kingdom – has, ruling over it, both a physical monarch and a spiritual ruler. Thus, if we are to be effective in our spiritual warfare – wrestling against both principalities and powers – we need to have a grasp on the principalities that govern our region – our state, county, city or

other political subdivision. Each kingdom and each political subdivision, has certain ruling demons that prevail. For example, over Babylon, it was the Mystery Religions; over Egypt was the spirit of bondage, over Greece, it was Philosophy, and over Rome was the spirit of death, manifest in the killing of tens of thousands of children and other thousands upon thousands, executed on stakes, or crosses, including our Lord and Savior, Jesus Christ.

Given this background, that each principality, or geographical region, has historically foisted particular types of persecution against those who sought to follow God, it seems important that we endeavor to discover what Principality and Powers rule over the cosmic forces within our region. Discovering these governing demonic entities is not easy, but it is usually not as difficult as it first seems. Often the local lore reveals those spiritual powers exercising authority. For example, the region where we now live has been called 'Poverty Flats' for generations; and as you might guess, the region has suffered economically while surrounding areas prosper.

Other areas – like San Francisco, California – are generally known as areas of sexual perversion; others – like New York, NY and Chicago, IL – are known as high crime areas; and some – like Sedona, AZ – are known to be centers of occult practice, yet few stop to consider that these sociological issues are but manifestations of the demonic forces assigned to that particular geographical area.

Occult Activities:
Another indicator of the particular demonic assignments over a region can be found by identifying the occult organizations and activities that dominate in the area. There are, as previously indicated, innumerable occult organizations – literally hundreds within the United States. Many of these operate in California where we reside. One is located very close to us – the Saint Germain Foundation – located on the slopes of Mount Shasta.

This, in and of itself is significant. Satan, after his fall declared: *"I will ascend to heaven; I will raise my throne above the stars of God; I will sit enthroned on the mount of assembly, on the utmost heights of the sacred mountain"* (Isa 14:13). First, we find the attempted construction of the Tower of Babel, whose builders said: *"Come, let us build ourselves a city, with a tower that reaches to the heavens, so that we may make a name for ourselves and not be scattered over the face of the whole earth"* (Gen 11:4).

174

Recognizing their true intent, *"The Lord came down to see the city and the tower that the men were building. The Lord said, "If as one people speaking the same language they have begun to do this, then nothing they plan to do will be impossible for them. Come, let us go down and confuse their language so they will not understand each other"* (Gen 11:5-7). Subsequent to this and, throughout the Old Testament, we find the powers of darkness, and those entrapped by them, seeking out the 'high places' as places of worship.

God understood their plan – their intent had never changed – so He declared: *"I will destroy your high places, cut down your incense altars and pile your dead bodies on the lifeless forms of your idols"* (Lev 26:30). But, again and again the nations surrounding Israel, built places of worship on the high places to worship demons. Finally, this practice even corrupted the Israelites. [they] *"built shrines on high places and appointed priests from all sorts of people, even though they were not Levites"* (1 Kings 12:31). This practice of idolatry finally reached the point that: *"Each national group made its own gods in the several towns where they settled, and set them up in the shrines the people of Samaria had made at the high places"* (2 Kings 17:29). And, while the nations that originated this practice are long gone, the practice remains.

High Places of Northern California:
Using the pattern given us – of geographic despots, or principalities; and high places of false worship – we need not look too far to discover its presence in our area. The Saint Germain Foundation is a religious organization, headquartered in Schaumburg, IL, a suburb of Chicago, that maintains a major facility just north of Dunsmuir, California, operating in the buildings and on the property of the Shasta Springs Retreat, located on the slopes of Mount Shasta. The organization also maintains a facility in the Capitol Hill neighborhood in downtown Denver, CO. The doctrines of the organization are based on teachings and 'wisdom' received by Guy Ballard, who claimed that while hiking on the slopes of Mount Shasta in 1930, a spirit-being who identified himself as Saint Germain appeared to him and began training him to be a "Messenger." The Ascended Master, Saint Germain is – among the occultists – known as "The God of Freedom" for the Earth and, since May 1, 1954, has supposedly been directing the Hierarchy for the "Dawning Golden Age" in this current Aquarian Age cycle. The name "Saint Germain" is the name that Francis Bacon allegedly chose to be his Ascended Master name following his alleged physical Ascension from the Rakoczy (Rákóczi) Mansion in Transylvania. The name comes from the Latin Sanctus Germanus, meaning "Holy Brother".

175

Ballard published his experiences in a series of books. The organization's philosophies became known as the "I AM Activity"; its members are popularly known as "I AM" Students. His alleged experiences are recorded in his books, **Unveiled Mysteries** and **The Magic Presence**, written under the pen name of Godfre Ray King. First published in 1934, the books have never been out of print.

This introduction was followed by more than 3000 Discourses allegedly given him by 'the Ascended Masters,' who – they themselves claim – are the dead, who have come back to instruct mankind. One – the primary entity – who allegedly referred to himself as Saint Germain, supposedly gave Mr. and Mrs. Ballard, daily directions, telling them that the purpose of the **Ascended Masters** was *"to bring humans help from their Octave [Dimension] of Life."*

Mankind – Saint Germain allegedly taught – must have more than ordinary assistance to stand against the accumulation of mankind's disobedience to the Laws of Life. Out of this came the idea that physical actions alone cannot solve the world's problems nor remove the discordant energy that human beings release against each other, usually ignorant of its immensely destructive force. The aim of the true seeker of the Light – the I AM-ers – is they say, to protect all that is constructive; and to maintain God (meaning Good) Ideals by dedicating one's Life to bring forth the Fulfillment of the Universal "Divine" Plan for all. This is based on our believing that we all have within ourselves christ-consciousness – which, if we will only listen to – will help us attain the level of Grand Master in this life, and Ascended Master after leaving this earth.

According to the group's teachings, Ascended Masters are believed to be individuals who have left the cycle of reincarnation, or re-embodiment. **The "I AM" Activity calls itself Christian, because Jesus is considered to be one of the more important Ascended Masters.** It also refers to itself as "patriotic" because Ascended Master Saint Germain is believed to have inspired and guided the creation of the Declaration of Independence and the Constitution while belonging to the same Masonic Lodge as George Washington and Benjamin Franklin, although Guy Ballard tended to downplay any relationship between his ideas and Freemasonry because of his great dislike, even hatred, of Franklin Delano Roosevelt, a famous Freemason.

Thus, the notion that the mystic figure Saint Germain belonged to a Masonic Lodge was more part of general occult lore than part of Ballard's emphasis.

The movement teaches that the omnipotent, omniscient and omnipresent creator God is the 'I AM' mentioned in Exodus 3:14, who is resident in all of us as a spark from the Divine Flame. They teach that we can experience this presence, this love, power and light – the power of the Violet Consuming Flame of Divine Love – through quiet contemplation and by repeating 'affirmations' and 'decrees'. They also believe that by 'affirming' something one desires, one can cause it to happen.

The group teaches that the "Mighty I AM Presence," is the way in which God exists as each person's Inner-being or Higher Self, and that a light known as the "Violet Flame" can be generated by the "I AM Presence" to surround each person who calls forth this action or expresses mercy, or forgiveness. The group believes that by tapping into these internalized, self-existent, powers in accordance with the teachings of the Ascended Masters, one can use the "Presence" to eliminate evil from the world in favor of justice, as well as to minimize one's own personal difficulties in life.

The spiritual goal of their teachings is that, through a process of self-purification, rather than ordinary death any believer may become an Ascended Master when leaving their body. The process of attaining these results includes meditation, affirmations, and "decrees", to create alignment with the "I AM Presence" and invoke the Violet Flame, resulting in the desired positive changes. The group also emphasizes personal freedoms, libertarian concepts, embracing patriotic symbols, and often displaying American flags in its Temples or other offices. These "positive thinking" beliefs overlap with several other New Age movements such as Religious Science and the Human Potential Movements.

Researchers studying the group have ranked it as an "established cult." The group was also labeled as cult in the 1995 Report of the Parliamentary Commission on Cults in France. The group founded a community in France in 1956, which is now located in the Alps. Worldwide, the cult boasted more than one million members in 1940, but began to decline after Ballard's death. Among the splinter groups of the Saint Germain Foundation, have been the Bridge to Freedom, The Summit Lighthouse, and the Church Universal and Triumphant.

Their goals and objectives may sound good, but the essential doctrine of the church – the I AM Activity – is that each of us is a 'god' in training; and **one of the principle activities of this "Church Universal and Triumphant" is to pray against the Christian Church; and they invoke demons to assist them in their goal.**

177

To gain a deeper understanding of the St. Germain Foundation, or I AM Society, one needs to read what someone, still involved in the occult, and very familiar with the group says about it.

"And, dominated by a woman dictator, this strange subversive cult has deceived and hypnotized so many; broken up homes; brought about divorces; caused insanities; blasphemed Christ; propagated lies; enunciated doctrines of hate; instilled nameless fear; bound thousands to psychic "Masters"; sent death blasts at the President of the United States; yet still continues in the United States of America, land of "religious" liberty. Strange, incredible, fantastic – pathetic, yet true --this is the story of that most extraordinary cult, known as the "Mighty I AM."

"The "I AM" cult claims that their philosophy is a combination all religions, although as you will see, the made up mythical "God" Saint Germain is only comparable to the most cruel of dogmatic religious figures. Is this the New Age Illuminati Religion which conspires to destroy individuality? One where the dogmatic fury of all religions is brought together to mind control its followers into a state of fear and subservience in a psychic dictatorship? I will leave such speculation up to you. Nonetheless, I will attempt to give my best explanation of why I see the "I AM"/Saint Germain and Ascended Masters Movement as a manipulative and deceptive cult, which is hijacking the creative powers (as well as wealth, health and happiness) of its followers through what I call a "Spiritual Trap".

"This past weekend I was invited by a loose group of friends to a free seminar in Denver, CO called "TAKE CHARGE OF YOUR LIFE" with Patricia Diane Cota-Robles. Although suspicious, I was compelled to go and take a look for a few hours. I was surprised to see that this seminar was particularly focused on discussing what you would call "New Age Philosophies", and it was packed full of people! Many concepts which were expressed in this seminar were very true and I resonated with the idea that we can change our life through our intentions.

"Although, it depends on what direction we want the world to change towards, as well as who is leading the movement. What are the goals and/or dreams of this cult? Are the intentions of these "Ascended Masters" benevolent ones? At the New Age Seminar I had an eery feeling that almost made me sick. It was a kind of psychic vampirism I experienced a few months ago while in a Catholic Cathedral. So when the leader of the free seminar told us to uncross our legs and let the energies of the "Mighty I AM" presence flow through our body, I intuitively left the room.

"Listening to less than decent music and praying to ascended masters made me suspicious that a psychological operation was underway. The dictator of the seminar Patricia Diane Cota-Robles continued throughout the rest of the seminar to talk about violet flames, the "Mighty I AM", and spirit of Saint Germain which we must open up to in order to save ourselves and the world."

Psychic Dictatorship in America, by Gerald Barbee Bryan.

Summary:

As Christians, we must be aware that Satan and his Kingdom of Darkness, endeavors in every way to counterfeit God's kingdom – the church. Its members aggressively pray against Christians, just as Christians are directed to pray against the demons – the powers of darkness – that influence them and their organization. We must stay focused on the direction provided by the apostle Paul:

"We are not wrestling with flesh and blood [contending only with physical opponents], but against the despotisms [principalities], against the powers, against [the master spirits who are] the world rulers of this present darkness, against the spirit forces of wickedness in the heavenly (supernatural) sphere" (Eph 6:12 AMP).

Every Christian called into spiritual warfare – as a Christians we all are – needs to invest the time and energy to undertake the research necessary to determine the Demonic Principality ruling over the area where we live, work and minister.

If you have never done such research, begin by looking through your local newspaper. What are the most common sociological problems reported? What are the majority of arrests for? How do the number of marriages compare with the number of divorces? How is your local city, county and state faring financially? What about the area's businesses?

Next, you might check with the intake person at the local Emergency Rooms [ER] at your local hospitals. What are the most prevailing presenting problems that bring individuals to the ER in your area? You may also wish to check out the vital statistics of your area – i.e., what are the death statistics pertaining to the age of death? How does this compare with the national and State average? What is the homeless rate of your area, and how does it compare with the national and State averages?

These statistics, and others you will think of, will help you develop pattern of the presenting problems affecting your area. With this, and keeping in mind the fact that we are not waging warfare with other humans, but with the principalities, ruling powers and cosmic forces of the kingdom of darkness; you should be able to begin identifying the ruling powers holding sway over your homeland.

With this information in hand, you and your fellow prayer warriors, will have the information necessary to commence resisting the powers of darkness that have, and are, attacking you – your home, church, workplace, and sociological systems.

Many of these 'ruling powers' mentioned by the Apostle Paul, are identified in Scripture and are referred to by certain researchers as the demonic 'strongmen'. We will be examining these in the succeeding chapters, but before we introduce these, it is imperative that we keep in mind that the commander of these demonic forces is called in the Hebrew tongue, Abaddon and in the Greek, Appolyon, both referring the Destroyer, or Satan.

Satan is the chief-counterfeiter, master of disguise and a superior strategist. He is the one who introduced the Nephilim onto the world stage; the prime-mover behind Nimrod and Semarimis in the construction of the Tower of Babel and the establishment of the Mystery Religions that all the world has followed after in amazement (Rev 13:3); the Chief Priest of the Synagogue of Satan. And, when under the New Covenant, God's chosen became indwelled by Holy Spirit, Satan was quick to imitate this by directing his demons – evil spirits – to infest the spirits of mankind.

Recognizing Satan's wily nature – his ability to improvise in order to compete with every plan and purpose of God – one should not limit the number, nor the identity, of the spiritual strongmen, or ruling powers, to those that are mentioned in Scripture. After all, prophecy tells us that in the last days Satan will perform great and miraculous signs and wonders.

Notwithstanding Satan's ability to improvise – to meet present circumstances and situations, and develop counterfeits that only the most discerning can identify as being ingenuous; we begin in volume two of this series, searching out the ruling powers over our era and culture, our family, and over our individual life, by examining the demonic strongmen mentioned by name in Scripture. Then, using this as a spring-board, we will examine other potential demonic strongmen that are active in our era and culture. Join us as we commence this interesting and important search.

Books by Dr. James V. & Mrs. Paula M. Potter

Waging Winning War in the Spirit Realm

This comprehensive landmark work on spiritual warfare is divided into four companion volumes:

- Volume One ~ Prepare For War ~ Personal Preparedness
- Volume Two ~ Spiritual Reconnaissance ~ Identifying The Enemy
- Volume Three ~ Engaging the Enemy ~ Successful Battle Plans
- Volume Four ~ Songs of Victory ~ Testimonies of Praise

Other Titles

Other titles by these authors you might find enjoyable and rewarding, include:

- God's Precious Promises: A Guide to Appropriating As Your Own, God's 8,000 + Promises

- Mysteries of The Bible: The Primeval Era ~ A Story of the Time When Giants Roamed the Earth

- Mysteries of the Bible: Armageddon ~ Christ & His Bride vs. The Antichrist & His Concubines [Iran with Gog & Magog; Radical Islam; MS-13 & MS-18]

- The Divine Exchange: Life for Life ~ Soul for Soul

- Our Spiritual Authority: Restoring the Power & Authority of the 1st. Century Church

- Soul Care: An Introduction to Pastoral Care

- Counseling Addicts & Offenders: A Guide to Criminal Justice Counseling

- Mastery Over Anger: Healing Relationships Through Constructive Conflict-Resolution

- Conquistando La Ira (Spanish Mastery Over Anger)

- Assertiveness, Individuation & Autonomy

- Conquering Codependency

- Jekyll & Hyde: Arrested Development & Personality Disorders

- Healing Inner-Child Wounds: Breaking Life Commandments

- Growing Beyond Our Genetics: Adolescence & Beyond

- Affair-Proofing Your Marriage: Bonding vs. Relationship Bondage

- Toxic Shame & The Journey Out

- Substances of Abuse: An ID & Symptom Guide

These volumes and other titles by Dr. James V. Potter and Paula M. Potter, MA; and other esteemed Christian authors publishing through Advocare Publishing Co., may be purchased through your local book store, or online through Amazon.com. To purchase online, go to our Amazon Store-Front by pasting the following link in your browser:

http://www.amazon.com/gp/search/ref=sr_gnr_fkmr1?rh=i%3Aaps%2Ck%3AAdvocare+Publishing&keywords=Advocare+Publishing&ie=UTF8&qid=1311691077

About the Authors

James V. Potter, Ph.D., and Paula M. Potter, MA – husband and wife – are Christian Authors, Educators, Pastoral Counselors and Ordained Ministers. Dr. and Paula Potter make their home in Northern California, where they retired in 2003 after decades in clinical pastoral counseling practice. Prior to their move to Northern California, they resided in Hawaii, on the Big Island.

There, the Potters served on the staff of the Family Ministry School, of the University of the Nations, a Division of Youth With A Mission; As Associate Pastors with the Gospel of Salvation Churches in Hilo, and the New Covenant Church in Waimea-Kamuela; and were engaged in private Clinical Pastoral Counseling.

Dr. James and Paula Potter, founded the Hawaii Family Care Centers – a network of community based, Christian Counseling Centers, serving at-risk individuals and families, ministering to substance abusers, addicts, domestic violence perpetrators and victims, and individuals struggling from various mood and personality disorders. Returning to California in 1995, Dr. Potter and Paula founded Agape Family Care Services and the Alliance Recovery Service, carrying on the clinical practice they had begun while in Hawaii.

After retiring from clinical practice in 2003, Dr. Potter and Paula founded Advocare Ministries, and its divisions: Advocare Publishing Co., to publish Christ-centered counseling resources, self-help guides and spiritual guidance materials; and Advocare Family Skills Institute, to carry on the work of training and equipping Christian Therapists, Counselors and Group Facilitators.

Through their affiliations with Vision Bible College and Vision International University, Dr. Potter and Paula mentor students in their bachelor and masters studies worldwide, through on-line instruction.

Dr. Potter and Paula are Certified Christian Marriage and Family Therapists; Certified Clinical Pastoral Counselors; Certified Domestic Violence and Abuse Prevention and Treatment Specialists; Certified Substance Abuse and Addiction Prevention and Treatment Specialists; and Certified Prepare/Enrich Counselors and Trainers.

Dr. Potter has been listed in numerous directories, including: Marquis, Who's Who in America, Who's Who in the World, Who's Who in Religion, and Who's Who in Education; Men of Achievement; the International Biographical Centre; Association for Christian Therapists; and the National Christian Counselors Association.

Dr. Potter is a member of the World Association for Online Education, and both Dr. Potter and Paula Potter serve as adjunct faculty for Vision International University, and teach in the Bonneyview Road Christian Center, Educational Programs, Redding, California.

WAGING WINNING WAR

IN THE SPIRIT REALM

Winning the Battle

For the weapons of our warfare are not carnal but **mighty in God** for pulling down strongholds, casting down arguments and every high thing that exalts itself against the knowledge of God, bringing every thought into captivity to the **Obedience of Christ.**

2 Corinthians 10:4,5

PART ONE

PREPARE FOR WAR

James V. Potter, Ph.D. & Paula M. Potter, MA
© 2011 Jubilee Enterprises
Advocare Publishing Co.
Anderson, California

WAGING WINNING WAR IN THE SPIRIT REALM

VOLUME ONE ~ PREPARE FOR WAR

ISBN: 1-930327-58-7   ISBN-13: 978-1-930327-58-0

Unless otherwise noted, all Biblical Scripture quotations in this volume are from the New International Version, Student Edition (NIV) Study Bible), copyright © 1985 by the Zondervan Corporation, Grand Rapids, Michigan, USA

ISBN: 1-930327-58-7   ISBN-13: 978-1-930327-58-0

Published by Advocare Publishing Co.
Anderson, California 96007-8207, USA

Printed in the United States of America

INTRODUCTION

Waging Winning War In The Spirit Realm ~ Part One: Prepare for War, is the initial volume of a series on spiritual warfare:

- Volume One ~ Prepare For War ~ Personal Preparedness
- Volume Two ~ Spiritual Reconnaissance ~ Identifying The Enemy
- Volume Three ~ Engaging the Enemy ~ Successful Battle Plans
- Volume Four ~ Songs of Victory ~ Testimonies of Praise

We live in a multi-dimensional reality, represented by our complex, holistic being of body, soul and spirit. These features of our complex being are governed by laws:

- Our body, or physical being, is governed by laws of physics, comprising our phenomenal reality – our reality that is based on the phenomena of our sensory information [sight, sound, smell, taste and touch.]

- Our soul – often referred to as our mind – is comprised of our intellect, affect [emotions], imagination, opinions, beliefs, attitudes, etc., comprise our psychological reality – our reality that is based on our internal thought processes and the integration of those processes, or the lack thereof.

- Our spirit – often referenced as our inner-being, or core – is comprised of things such as our spiritual orientation, our sexual identity, our volition or will, our core-values and life-commandments. These comprise our spiritual reality, usually spoken of as our spirituality.

Most are quite familiar with the basic laws of physics as well as those of psychology, rarely questioning the fact that there are indeed laws that govern our body [physical reality] and our soul [psychological reality]. Surprisingly, however, many who are quite familiar with these laws are equally unfamiliar with the laws that govern our spirit and our interaction with the spirit world [or spiritual reality].

The Apostle Paul, speaking of this dimension, or reality, and the laws governing it said: *"Finally, grow powerful in union with the Lord, in union with his mighty strength! Use all the armor and weaponry that God provides, so that you will be able to stand against the deceptive tactics of the Adversary. For we are not struggling against human beings, but against the rulers, authorities and cosmic powers governing this darkness, against the spiritual forces of evil in the heavenly realm.*

So take up every piece of war equipment God provides; so that when the evil day comes, you will be able to resist; and when the battle is won, you will still be standing. Therefore, stand! Have the belt of **truth buckled around** *your* **waist, put on righteousness for a breastplate,** *and wear on your* **feet the readiness that comes from the Good News of** *shalom. Always carry the shield of trust, with which you will be able to extinguish all the flaming arrows of the Evil One. And take* **the helmet of deliverance;** *along with the sword given by the Spirit, that is, the Word of God; as you pray at all times, with all kinds of prayers and requests, in the Spirit, vigilantly and persistently, for all God's people.* (Eph 6:10-18 CJB).

It is this spiritual realm that Paul is describing when he wrote: *"I pray that he will give light to the eyes of your hearts, so that you will understand the hope to which he has called you, what rich glories there are in the inheritance he has promised his people, and how surpassingly great is his power working in us who trust him. It works with the same mighty strength he used when* **He worked in the Messiah to raise him from the dead and seat him at his right hand in heaven, far above every ruler, authority, power, dominion or any other name that can be named either in the 'olam hazeh [present age and culture or in the 'olam haba [one to come].** *Also,* **He has put all things under his feet and made him head over everything for the Messianic Community, which is his body, the full expression of him who fills all creation"** (Eph 1:18-23 CJB).

It is this realm that those who are born-again and are in spirit-to-Spirit union with Christ Jesus occupy. *"God raised us up with the Messiah Yeshua and seated us with him in heaven, in order to exhibit in the ages to come how infinitely rich is his grace, how great is his kindness toward us who are united with the Messiah Yeshua"* (Eph 2:6-8 CJB). It is this realm in which the Church of Christ primarily functions; it is wherel the unholy entities intent on the church's destruction dwell (Eph 3:10); and the realm where mortal spiritual battle rages.